QUESTIONS
ABOUT THE
BIBLE

QUESTIONS ABOUT THE BIBLE

THE 100 MOST FREQUENTLY ASKED QUESTIONS ABOUT THE BIBLE

S. MICHAEL HOUDMANN
GENERAL EDITOR

WESTBOW·
PRESS
A DIVISION OF THOMAS NELSON
& ZONDERVAN

WestBow Press books may be ordered through booksellers or by contacting:

WestBow Press
A Division of Thomas Nelson & Zondervan
1663 Liberty Drive
Bloomington, IN 47403
www.westbowpress.com
1 (866) 928-1240

ISBN: 978-1-4908-7800-3 (sc)
ISBN: 978-1-4908-7801-0 (e)

Library of Congress Control Number: 2015906509

Print information available on the last page.

WestBow Press rev. date: 6/3/2015

CONTENTS

ACKNOWLEDGEMENTS

THIS BOOK IS dedicated to the more than 500 individuals who have served as volunteer writers for Got Questions Ministries in the past thirteen years. Their hard work, commitment, and passion are what make this ministry possible.

Special thanks goes to Kevin Stone, Rebekah Largent, MeLissa Houdmann, Kristi-Joy Matovich, and Gwen Sellers who contributed greatly to this volume in writing, editing, organizing, and indexing.

All the glory goes to God, "For from him and through him and to him are all things. To him be the glory forever! Amen." (Romans 11:36)

PREFACE

E VERY DAY, MORE and more people turn to the Internet to find answers to their questions about spiritual matters. Topics related to spirituality are the second-most searched subjects online. Sadly, websites that present false teachings far outnumber those that proclaim the truth of God's Word.

In February of 2002, www.gotquestions.org was launched to help fill this gap and meet the needs of millions of spiritually-minded Web surfers. Since our launch, we have personally answered over 420,000 questions that have been submitted to us. Tens of millions of people have found answers to their questions via our Frequently Asked Questions archives, giving us a unique understanding of what questions are truly on people's minds.

This volume is a collection of the most important and/or most frequently asked questions about the Bible. Each question is answered directly from the Bible, if the Bible specifically addresses the particular issue. Where the Bible is silent on an issue, biblical principles are used to lead to a solid and correct understanding. The Lord Jesus Christ is our passion, and declaring His Word is our mission.

Mission Statement of Got Questions Ministries:

Got Questions Ministries seeks to glorify the Lord Jesus Christ by providing biblical, applicable, and timely answers to spiritually-related questions.

Introduction— The Ultimate Question

Question: What does it mean to be a born-again Christian?

Answer: What does it mean to be a born-again Christian? The classic passage from the Bible that answers this question is John 3:1–21. The Lord Jesus Christ is talking to Nicodemus, a prominent Pharisee and member of the Sanhedrin (the ruling body of the Jews). Nicodemus had come to Jesus at night with some questions.

As Jesus talked with Nicodemus, He said, "'I tell you the truth, no one can see the kingdom of God unless he is born again.' 'How can a man be born when he is old?' Nicodemus asked. 'Surely he cannot enter a second time into his mother's womb to be born!' Jesus answered, 'I tell you the truth, no one can enter the kingdom of God unless he is born of water and the Spirit. Flesh gives birth to flesh, but the Spirit gives birth to spirit. You should not be surprised at my saying, "You must be born again"'" (John 3:3–7).

The phrase "born again" could be literally translated "born from above." Nicodemus had a real need. He needed a change of his heart—a spiritual transformation. New birth—being born again—is an act of God whereby eternal life is imparted to the person who believes (2 Corinthians 5:17; Titus 3:5; 1 Peter 1:3; 1 John 2:29; 3:9; 4:7; 5:1–4). John 1:12–13 indicates that being "born again" also carries the idea of "becoming children of God" through trust in the name of Jesus Christ.

The question logically comes, "Why does a person need to be born again?" The apostle Paul in Ephesians 2:1 says, "And you He made alive, who were dead in trespasses and sins" (NKJV). To the Romans he wrote, "For all have sinned and fall short of the glory of God" (Romans 3:23). Sinners are spiritually "dead"; when they receive spiritual life through faith in Christ, the Bible likens it to a rebirth. Only those who are born again have their sins forgiven and have a relationship with God.

How does that come to be? Ephesians 2:8–9 states, "For it is by grace you have been saved, through faith—and this not from yourselves, it is the gift of God—not by works, so that no one can boast." When one is saved, he/she has been born again, spiritually renewed, and is now a child of God by right of new birth. Trusting in Jesus Christ, the One who paid the penalty of sin when He died on the cross, is the means to be "born again." "Therefore, if anyone is in Christ, he is a new creation; the old has gone, the new has come!" (2 Corinthians 5:17).

If you have never trusted in the Lord Jesus Christ as your Savior, will you consider the prompting of the Holy Spirit as He speaks to your heart? You need to be born again. Will you pray the prayer of repentance and become a new creation in Christ today? "Yet to all who received him, to those who believed in his name, he gave the right to become children of God—children born not of natural descent, nor of human decision or a husband's will, but born of God" (John 1:12–13).

If you want to accept Jesus Christ as your Savior and be born again, here is a sample prayer. Remember, saying this prayer or any other prayer will not save you. It is only trusting in Christ that can save you from sin. This prayer is simply a way to express to God your faith in Him and thank Him for providing for your salvation. "God, I know that I have sinned against you and am deserving of punishment. But Jesus Christ took the punishment I deserve so that through faith in Him I could be forgiven. I place my trust in You for salvation. Thank You for Your wonderful grace and forgiveness—the gift of eternal life! Amen!"

Have you made a decision to receive Jesus Christ as your Savior because of what you have read here? If so, please send us an email at questions@gotquestions.org.

Chapter 1

QUESTIONS ABOUT THE BIBLE'S ORIGIN

Contents

Question: What is the Bible?

Answer: The word *Bible* comes from the Latin and Greek words meaning "book," a fitting name, since the Bible is the book for all people, for all time. It's a book like no other, in a class by itself.

Sixty-six different books comprise the Bible. They include books of law, such as Leviticus and Deuteronomy; historical books, such as Ezra and Acts; books of poetry, such as Psalms and Ecclesiastes; books of prophecy, such as Isaiah and Revelation; biographies, such as Matthew and John; and epistles (formal letters) such as Titus and Hebrews.

The Authors

About 40 different human authors contributed to the Bible, which was written over a period of about 1,500 years. The authors were kings, fishermen, priests, government officials, farmers, shepherds, and doctors. From all this diversity comes an incredible unity, with common themes woven throughout.

The Bible's unity is due to the fact that, ultimately, it has one Author—God Himself. The Bible is "God-breathed" (2 Timothy 3:16). The human authors wrote exactly what God wanted them to write, and the result was the perfect and holy Word of God (Psalm 12:6; 2 Peter 1:21).

The Divisions

The Bible is divided into two main parts: the Old Testament and the New Testament. In short, the Old Testament is the story of a nation, and the New Testament is the story of a Man. The nation was God's way of bringing the Man—Jesus Christ—into the world.

The Old Testament describes the founding and preservation of the nation of Israel. God promised to use Israel to bless the whole world (Genesis 12:2–3). Once Israel was established as a nation, God raised up a family within that nation through whom the blessing would come: the family of David (Psalm 89:3–4). God promised one Man from the family of David who would bring the promised blessing (Isaiah 11:1–10).

The New Testament details the coming of that promised Man. His name was Jesus, and He fulfilled the prophecies of the Old Testament as He lived a perfect life, died to become the Savior, and rose from the dead.

The Central Character

Jesus is the central character in the Bible—the whole book is really about Him. The Old Testament predicts His coming and sets the stage for His entrance into the world. The New Testament describes His coming and His work to bring salvation to our sinful world.

Jesus is more than a historical figure; in fact, He is more than a man. He is God in the flesh, and His coming was the most important event in the history of the world. God Himself became a man in order to give us a clear, understandable picture of who He is. What is God like? He is like Jesus; Jesus is God in human form (John 1:14; 14:9).

A Brief Summary

God created man and placed him in a perfect environment; however, man rebelled against God and fell from what God intended him to be. God placed the world under a curse because of sin but immediately set in motion a plan to restore humanity and all creation to its original glory.

As part of His plan of redemption, God called Abraham out of Babylonia into Canaan (about 2000 BC). God promised Abraham, his son Isaac, and his grandson Jacob (also called Israel) that He would bless the world through a descendant of theirs. Israel's family emigrated from Canaan to Egypt, where they grew to be a nation.

Around 1400 BC, God led Israel's descendants out of Egypt under the direction of Moses and gave them the Promised Land, Canaan, as their own. Through Moses, God gave the people of Israel the Law and made a covenant (testament) with them. If they would remain faithful to God and not follow the idolatry of the surrounding nations, then they would prosper. If they forsook God and followed idols, then God would destroy their nation.

About 400 years later, during the reigns of David and his son Solomon, Israel was solidified into a great and powerful kingdom. God promised David and Solomon that a descendant of theirs would rule as an everlasting king.

After Solomon's reign, the nation of Israel was divided. The ten tribes to the north were called Israel, and they lasted about 200 years before God judged them for their idolatry. Assyria took Israel captive about 721 BC. The two tribes in the south were called Judah, and they lasted a little longer; but eventually they, too, turned from God. Babylon took them captive around 600 BC.

About 70 years later, God graciously brought a remnant of the captives back into their own land. Jerusalem, the capital, was rebuilt about 444 BC, and Israel once again established a national identity. Thus, the Old Testament closes.

The New Testament opens nearly 400 years later with the birth of Jesus Christ in Bethlehem. Jesus was the descendant promised to Abraham and David, the One to fulfill God's plan to redeem mankind and restore creation. Jesus faithfully completed His work—He died for sin and rose from the dead. The death of Christ is the basis for a new covenant with the world. All who have faith in Jesus will be saved from sin and live eternally with Him.

After His resurrection, Jesus sent His disciples to spread the news of His life and His power to save. Jesus' disciples went in every direction, preaching the good news of Jesus and salvation. They traveled through Asia Minor, Greece, and all the Roman Empire. The New Testament closes with a prediction of Jesus' return to judge the unbelieving world and free creation from the curse.

Question: Who were the authors of the books of the Bible?

Answer: Ultimately, God is the true author of the Bible. Second Timothy 3:16 tells us that the Bible was "breathed" by God. God superintended the human authors of the Bible so that, while using their own writing styles and personalities, they still recorded exactly what God intended. God did not dictate the Bible, but it was perfectly guided and entirely inspired by Him.

Humanly speaking, the Bible was written by approximately 40 men of diverse backgrounds over the course of 1,500 years. Isaiah was a prophet, Ezra was a priest, Matthew was a tax collector, John was a fisherman, Paul was a tentmaker, Moses was a shepherd, and Luke was a physician. Despite being penned by different authors over 15 centuries, the Bible does not contradict itself and does not contain any errors. The authors all present different perspectives, but they all proclaim the same one true God and the same one way of salvation—Jesus Christ (John 14:6; Acts 4:12).

Few of the books of the Bible specifically name their author, but we are able to compile the following list of probable authors, along with the approximate date of authorship:

Genesis, Exodus, Leviticus, Numbers, Deuteronomy
Moses; 1400 BC

Joshua
Joshua; 1350 BC

Judges, Ruth, 1 Samuel, 2 Samuel
Samuel/Nathan/Gad; 1000–900 BC

1 Kings, 2 Kings
Jeremiah; 600 BC

1 Chronicles, 2 Chronicles, Ezra, Nehemiah
Ezra; 450 BC

Esther
Mordecai; 400 BC

Job
Moses; 1400 BC

Psalms
several different authors, mostly David; 1000–400 BC

Proverbs, Ecclesiastes, Song of Solomon
Solomon; 900 BC

Isaiah
Isaiah; 700 BC

Jeremiah, Lamentations
Jeremiah; 600 BC

Ezekiel
Ezekiel; 550 BC

Daniel
Daniel; 550 BC

Hosea
Hosea; 750 BC

Joel
Joel; 850 BC

Amos
Amos; 750 BC

Obadiah
Obadiah; 600 BC

Jonah
Jonah; 700 BC

Micah
Micah; 700 BC

Nahum
Nahum; 650 BC

Habakkuk
Habakkuk; 600 BC

Zephaniah
Zephaniah; 650 BC

Haggai
Haggai; 520 BC

Zechariah
Zechariah; 500 BC

Malachi
Malachi; 430 BC

Matthew
Matthew; AD 55

Mark
John Mark; AD 50

Luke
Luke; AD 60

John
John; AD 90

Acts
Luke; AD 65

Romans, 1 Corinthians, 2 Corinthians, Galatians, Ephesians, Philippians, Colossians, 1 Thessalonians, 2 Thessalonians, 1 Timothy, 2 Timothy, Titus, Philemon
Paul; AD 50–70

Hebrews
unknown, mostly likely Paul, Luke, Barnabas, or Apollos; AD 65

James
James; AD 45

1 Peter, 2 Peter
Peter; AD 60

1 John, 2 John, 3 John
John; AD 90

Jude
Jude; AD 60

Revelation
John; AD 90

Question: How do we know when the books of the Bible were written?

Answer: We have some basic ways of knowing when the individual books of the Bible were written through a combination of internal and external evidence and, particularly in the Old Testament, traditional accounts.

Internal evidence might consist of the style of writing and references to people or places that can be precisely dated. For example, while the story of Ruth is *set* during the time of the judges, scholars place the *writing* of the story in the time of the monarchy based on Ruth's literary style compared to other writings dated to that time. The mention of David in Ruth 4:17, 22 also strongly implies that Ruth was written sometime during or after David's reign.

Another example: the book of Daniel uses a literary style and specific Persian and Greek words that place it around the time of Cyrus the Great (ca. 530 BC). Linguistic evidence from the Dead Sea Scrolls gives us authentically dated examples of Hebrew and

Aramaic writing from the second and third centuries BC, when some claim Daniel was written, and it does not match that found in Daniel, which was written in the sixth century BC.

Other internal evidence might include the concerns the author is addressing. For example, the two books of Chronicles tell the history of the Jewish people and how they came under God's judgment in the form of the exile to Babylon. Traditionally, scholars have believed Ezra to be the author of these books, because the following two books, Ezra and Nehemiah (also written by Ezra), deal with the return from exile and the need to be obedient to God's Law. First and Second Chronicles, Ezra, and Nehemiah are written in nearly the same literary style, have a common goal, and relate a single narrative.

The date of Israel's return from exile, which began under Cyrus the Great, can be correlated to independent historical records that place his reign from approximately 559 to 530 BC. The records of Darius I corroborate the dedication of the new temple in Jerusalem in 516 BC, and a second return of exiles was allowed under Artaxerxes I, whom we know ruled Babylon from 465 to 424 BC. All these things help us to know the time that Ezra wrote his books. Biblical scholars use similar cross-referencing to date other books of the Old Testament.

In the New Testament, books are generally dated by the concerns being addressed (such as the growing Gnostic heresy), how much they quote from other New Testament writings, and a cross-referencing of events (such as the collection for the needy in Jerusalem, mentioned in Romans and 1 and 2 Corinthians). We also have historical, extra-biblical accounts from men such as Flavius Josephus to corroborate events described in the Bible.

The Gospels are often dated by something that is *not* mentioned: Jesus predicted the fall of Jerusalem in Matthew 24:1–2, and we know from history that the city fell in AD 70. It seems logical that, if such a prominent prophecy had been fulfilled before the writing of the Gospels, it would have been mentioned by the gospel writers. Other prophecies are mentioned with their fulfillments (e.g.,

John 2:19, 22); the non-inclusion of Jerusalem's fall suggests that Matthew wrote his gospel before AD 70.

It's important to note that, even among scholars who believe the Bible to be God's inspired Word, there is some disagreement as to the exact dating of the biblical books. A good study Bible or commentary will lay out the various lines of evidence for the dating of the books.

Question: When were the Gospels written?

Answer: None of the Gospels include a dateline. So, the dating of the Gospels and other New Testament books is at best an educated guess and at worst foolish speculation. For example, suggested dates for the writing of the gospel of Matthew range from as early as AD 40 to as late as AD 140. This wide range of dates from scholars indicates the subjective nature of the dating process. Generally, one will find that the presuppositions of the scholars greatly influence their dating of the Gospels.

For example, many liberal theologians have argued for a later dating of many New Testament books in an attempt to discredit or cast doubt upon the content and authenticity of the gospel accounts. On the other hand, there are many scholars who look to a much earlier dating of the New Testament books. There is good evidence to support the view that the whole New Testament, including Revelation, was written prior to the destruction of Jerusalem in AD 70. It is our contention that the evidence supports the earlier dating more than it does the later dating.

There are scholars who believe the gospel of Matthew was written as early as 10 to 12 years after the death of Christ. Those who hold to this earlier dating of Matthew believe he first wrote his gospel in Aramaic, and then it was later translated into Greek. One of the evidences of this earlier dating of Matthew's gospel is that early church leaders such as Irenaeus, Origen, and Eusebius recorded that Matthew wrote his gospel for Jewish believers while he was still in Palestine. In fact, Eusebius (a bishop of Caesarea and known as the father of church history) reported that Matthew wrote his gospel before he left Palestine to preach in other lands, which Eusebius says happened about 12 years after the death of Christ. This would place the writing of Matthew as early as AD 40–45.

Even if the Gospels were not written until 30 years after Christ's death, that would still place their writing prior to the destruction of Jerusalem in AD 70. This presents no major problem for their authority or accuracy. Even at that time there would have been a considerable number of eyewitnesses around to dispute any false claims. Also, the fact that none of the "hard sayings" of Jesus were taken from the gospel accounts supports their accuracy. Had the Gospels been "edited" before being written down, as some liberal scholars contend, then it was a very poor job. The gospel writers include far too many "hard sayings," cultural bombshells, and politically incorrect accounts. For example, the first witnesses of the resurrection were women, who were not considered reliable witnesses in the culture of that day.

The bottom line for Christians is this: whether the Gospels were written soon after the death of Christ or 30 years after that does not really matter, because their accuracy and authority do not rest on when they were written but on what they are—the divinely inspired Word of God (2 Timothy 3:16). One of the promises Jesus gave His disciples was that He would send them "another helper," the Holy Spirit, who would teach them all things and "remind you of everything I have said to you" (John 14:26). We can have total confidence and faith in the Gospels' completeness and accuracy, knowing they were written by men "carried along by the Holy Spirit" (2 Peter 1:21), who accurately recorded the very words of God.

Question: Did the Bible copy some of its stories from other religious myths and legends?

Answer: There are many stories in the Bible that have remarkable similarities with stories from other religions, legends, and myths.

For the purposes of this article, we will examine two of the more prominent examples.

First, let's consider the account of the fall of mankind into sin (Genesis 3). There is a Greek legend, that of Pandora's Box, wherein the details differ so dramatically from the biblical account of the fall that one might never suspect a relationship. But they may actually attest to the same historical event. Both stories tell how the very first woman unleashed sin, sickness, and suffering upon the world, which had been, up to that point, an Edenic paradise. Both stories end with the emergence of hope—hope in a promised Redeemer in the case of Genesis, and "hope" as a thing having been released from the box at the very end of the Pandora legend.

Like the world's copious flood legends, Pandora's Box demonstrates how the Bible might parallel pagan myths at times simply because they all speak of a historical core truth that has over the years manifested itself in ancient histories (as in the case of the Bible) and in poetic allegories (as in the case of Pandora, whose story was told in many different ways by the Greeks but whose core truth remained fairly constant). The similarities do not point to one account copying from the other, but to the fact that both stories point back to the same historical event.

Finally, there *are* cases of borrowing—but in these cases, the Bible was the source, not the pagan myths (despite pseudo-academic claims to the contrary). Consider the case of Sargon's birth. Legend has it that Sargon (an Akkadian emperor born in the 23rd century BC) was placed in a reed basket and sent down the river by his mother. He was rescued by Aqqi, who then adopted him as his own son. That sounds a lot like the story Moses in Exodus 2. And Sargon lived about 800 years before Moses was born. So the Moses baby-sent-down-the-river-only-to-be-rescued-and-adopted story must have been borrowed from Sargon, right?

That sounds reasonable, but what is known of Sargon comes almost entirely from legends written many hundreds of years *after* his death. There are very few contemporary records of Sargon's life. The legend of Sargon's childhood, how he was placed in a basket and sent down a river, comes from two seventh-century BC cuneiform tablets (from the library of the Assyrian king Ashurbanipal, who reigned from 668 to 627 BC), written hundreds of years after the book of Exodus. If someone wants to argue that one account was borrowed from another, it would have to be that the Sargon legend was borrowed from the Exodus account of Moses.

The Bible is clear as to its authorship. Although many different men wrote, the Holy Spirit of God is the actual author. Second Timothy 3:16 tells us that Scripture is inspired by God, which means it is "God-breathed." He wrote it, He preserved it through the centuries, He lives within its very pages, and through it His power is manifest in our lives.

Question: What are the Dead Sea Scrolls, and why are they important?

Answer: The first of the Dead Sea Scroll discoveries occurred in 1947 in Qumran, a village situated about 20 miles east of Jerusalem on the northwest shore of the Dead Sea. A young Bedouin shepherd, following a goat that had gone astray, tossed a rock into one of the caves along the sea cliffs and heard a cracking sound: the rock had hit a ceramic pot containing leather and papyrus scrolls that were later determined to be nearly 20 centuries old. Ten years and many searches later, 11 caves around the Dead Sea were found to contain tens of thousands of scroll fragments dating from the third century BC to AD 68 and representing an estimated 800 separate works.

The Dead Sea Scrolls comprise a vast collection of Jewish documents written in Hebrew, Aramaic, and Greek and encompass many subjects and literary styles. They include manuscripts or fragments of every book in the Hebrew Bible except the Book of Esther, all of them created nearly 1,000 years earlier than any previously known biblical manuscripts. The scrolls also contain the earliest existing biblical commentary (on the book of Habakkuk) and many other writings, among them religious works pertaining to Jewish sects of the time.

The legends of what was contained in the Dead Sea Scrolls are far beyond what was actually there. There were no lost books of the

Bible or other literature that did not already have existing copies. The vast majority of the Dead Sea Scrolls were simply copies of books of the Old Testament, dating from 250–150 BC.

The Dead Sea Scrolls were an amazing discovery in that the scrolls were in excellent condition and had remained hidden for so long (over 2,000 years). The Dead Sea Scrolls can also give us confidence in the reliability of the Old Testament manuscripts, since there were minimal differences between the manuscripts that had previously been discovered and those that were found in Qumran. Clearly, this is a testament to the way God has preserved His Word down through the centuries, protecting it from extinction and guarding it against significant error.

Question: How did the things Jesus said and did when He was alone get recorded in the Gospels?

Answer: There are a number of times in the Gospels when Jesus' words are quoted or His actions are described during times when He was alone. For example, when Jesus was in the desert for 40 days (Matthew 4) or praying in the Garden at Gethsemane (Mark 14), He was by Himself. How did anyone know what He said or did, since there were no eyewitnesses to what happened?

The gospel narratives were not written at the time the events happened, like some kind of daily journal entry; rather, they were put together later, like most historical narratives, based on memory, research, and compilation. Matthew and John were both eyewitnesses to most of the events in their narratives. Mark and Luke had access to the eyewitnesses. In fact, Luke mentions that he "carefully investigated everything from the beginning" before writing his gospel (Luke 1:3). It's probable that Mark gleaned information for his gospel from the apostle Peter (1 Peter 5:13). The other benefit the writers had—and this is a big one—is that they were inspired by the Holy Spirit (2 Timothy 3:16). In fact, Jesus had promised them that the Spirit would bring to their remembrance "everything I have said" (John 14:26).

Still, how did the disciples know what transpired when they were away from Jesus? One possible explanation is that the Holy Spirit told them what happened as they were writing their histories. Believing the Gospels to be inspired, we can easily accept that explanation.

Another explanation is simply that Jesus later told His disciples what they had missed. No disciple was present with Jesus during the wilderness temptation in Matthew 4, but after that Jesus spent over three years with the disciples. Isn't it likely that He related to them what had happened sometime during those three years? Similarly, Jesus was alone as He spoke to the woman at the well in John 4, yet their conversation is quoted at length. A common-sense explanation is that Jesus later filled in His disciples. Or perhaps John got the story from the woman, given the fact that the disciples stayed in her city for two days following her conversion (John 4:40).

After His resurrection, Jesus appeared to the disciples over a period of 40 days "speaking to them about the kingdom of God" (Acts 1:3). In those 40 days, Jesus would have had ample opportunity to inform the disciples of all the things that had happened to Him when they were not around. In any case, the events of Jesus' life that God wanted us to know—including events that occurred in solitude—were documented. The key is *God wanted us to know.* Either the events were disclosed directly to the disciples at a later time, by Jesus or by someone else, or the apostles learned the details straight from the Holy Spirit as they wrote God's Word.

Question: Is the original Bible still in existence?

Answer: The answer to this question is both "no" and "yes." In the strictest sense, no, the original documents that comprise the 66 books of the Bible—sometimes called the *autographs*—are not in the possession of any organization. However, in a very real way, yes, humankind does have the actual words and books that make up the Word of God. How can this be? To gain an understanding of how the original Bible was written and how it compares to what is read today, it is necessary to look at the process of its original compilation and what has happened since that time.

Background of the Original Bible

According to skeptics, there has never been a true "original" Bible. For example, Dan Brown's fictional book *The Da Vinci Code* has his story's "expert" say the following about the Bible: "The Bible did not arrive by fax from heaven. . . . The Bible is the product of man, my dear. Not of God. The Bible did not fall magically from the clouds. Man created it as a historical record of tumultuous times, and it has evolved through countless translations, additions, and revisions. History has never had a definitive version of the book."[1] Brown's charge does indeed belong in a work of fiction because the assertion is simply not true.

It is correct that the Bible was written over a long period of time. Written by 40 authors over a period of some 1,500 years, the Scriptures are made up of 66 books—39 in the Old Testament and 27 in the New. The Old Testament is oftentimes divided into three sections: 1) the Pentateuch, which is sometimes referred to as "The Law" and includes the first five books of the Bible; 2) the Prophets, which includes all the major and minor prophetic writings; and 3) the Writings, which includes Psalms, Proverbs, and a number of other books.

The New Testament is also divided into three segments: 1) the Gospels; 2) Church History, which basically is just the book of Acts; and 3) the Apostolic Writings, which includes everything else.

Compilation of the Original
Old Testament

How was the original Bible as described above compiled? Its assemblage can be traced through Scripture. After Moses wrote the Pentateuch (Exodus 17:14; 24:4, 7; 34:27; Numbers 33:2; Matthew 19:8; John 5:46–47; Romans 10:5), it was placed in the Holy of Holies and preserved (Deuteronomy 31:24–26). Over time, other inspired texts were added to the first five books of the Bible.

During the time of David and Solomon, the books already compiled were placed in the temple treasury (1 Kings 8:6) and cared for by the priests who served in the temple (2 Kings 22:8). More books were added during the reign of King Hezekiah—David's hymns, Solomon's proverbs, and prophetic books such as Isaiah, Hosea, and Micah (Proverbs 25:1). In general, as the prophets of God spoke and their words were written down, they were included in what today is the Old Testament.

During the Israeli exile in the sixth century BC, the books were scattered, but not lost. Around 539 BC and after the return of Israel from the Babylonian captivity, Ezra the priest re-collected all of the books and added other works to the compilation. They were then stored in the ark that was constructed for the second temple and meticulously copied to preserve the inspired writings. This collection of Old Testament books, written in Hebrew, is what Judaism calls the "Hebrew Bible."

In the third century BC, the Old Testament books were translated into Greek by a team of 70 Jewish scholars. This translation is called the Septuagint (a Latin word derived from the phrase "the translation of the seventy interpreters"), abbreviated as LXX ("70"). The Septuagint was used and quoted by the apostles in their writings. The oldest manuscripts of the LXX include some first- and second-century BC fragments.

In 1947, the Dead Sea Scrolls were discovered in the area of Qumran in Israel and dated anywhere from the fifth century BC to the first century AD. Historians believe that Jewish scribes maintained the site to preserve God's Word, especially during the destruction of Jerusalem in AD 70. The Dead Sea Scrolls represent nearly every book of the Old Testament, and comparisons with later manuscripts show them to be virtually identical, with the main deviations being the spellings of names and various numbers.

Luke records a statement of Jesus regarding the extent of the Old Testament: "This generation will be held responsible for the blood of all the prophets that has been shed since the beginning of the world, *from the blood of Abel to the blood of Zechariah*, who was killed between the altar and the sanctuary" (Luke 11:50–51, emphasis added). Jesus confirmed the 39 books of the Old Testament in these verses. Abel's death is found in Genesis, the first book; and Zechariah's in 2 Chronicles, the last book in the Hebrew Bible. Saying, "From Abel to Zechariah," was the equivalent of saying, "From beginning to end." Thus, Jesus considered the canon of the Old Testament as a unified whole.

Compilation of the Original New Testament

Dan Burstein, in his book *Secrets of the Code* (a book similar to Dan Brown's book), says this about the New Testament: "Eventually, four Gospels and twenty-three other texts were canonized into a Bible. This did not occur, however, until the sixth century."[2] Is this assertion true? Actually, it is 100 percent false. The truth is the composition of the New Testament was officially settled at the Council of Carthage in AD 397. However, the majority of the New Testament was accepted as authoritative much earlier. A man named Marcion proposed the first collection of New Testament books in AD 140. Marcion was a docetist (docetism is a system of belief that says all spirit is good and all material matter is bad), and so Marcion excluded any book that spoke of Jesus being both divine and human, and he also edited Paul's letters to match his own philosophy.

The next proposed collection of New Testament books on record was the Muratorian Canon, dated AD 170. It included all four gospels; Acts; 13 of Paul's letters; 1, 2, 3 John; Jude; and Revelation. The final New Testament canon was identified by the church father Athanasius in AD 367 and ratified by the Council of Carthage in AD 397.

But history shows that today's New Testament was recognized much earlier and does, in fact, accurately reflect what the "autographs" contained. First, Scripture itself shows that the writings of the New Testament were considered inspired at the time of their writing. For example, Paul writes, "For the Scripture says, 'Do not muzzle the ox while it is treading out the grain,' and *'The worker deserves his wages'*" (1 Timothy 5:18, emphasis added). The latter quotation is from Luke 10:7, which Paul calls "Scripture." Another example: "Bear in mind that our Lord's patience means salvation, just as our dear brother Paul also wrote you with the wisdom that God gave him. He writes the same way in all his letters, speaking in them of these matters. His letters contain some things that are hard to understand, which ignorant and unstable people distort, as they do *the other Scriptures*, to their own destruction" (2 Peter 3:15-16, emphasis added). It is clear that Peter regarded Paul's letter as equally inspired as the Old Testament canon.

Also, we have quotations from the early church fathers that would allow the reconstruction of almost the entire New Testament as it is found today. For example, Clement (circa AD 95) quotes from 11 New Testament books, Ignatius (circa AD 107) quotes from nearly every New Testament book, and Polycarp (a disciple of John, circa AD 110) quotes from 17 New Testament books. Just using early church fathers' quotes, the entire New Testament can be pieced together with the exception of twenty-some verses, most of them from 3 John. Such evidence witnesses to the fact that the New Testament was recognized far before the Council of Carthage in AD 397 and that our New Testament today reflects what was written 2,000 years ago.

There is no literary rival in the ancient world to the number of manuscript copies and the early dating of the New Testament. There are 5,300 Greek, 10,000 Latin, and 9,000 miscellaneous copies of the New Testament that exist today, and more continue to be unearthed via archaeology. The combination of early dating and the enormous number of New Testament copies causes historical experts such as Sir Frederic Kenyon (former director/principal librarian of the British Museum) to say, "The interval, then, between the dates of original composition and the earliest extant evidence becomes so small as to be in fact negligible, and the last foundation for any doubt that the Scriptures have come down to us substantially as they were written has now been removed. Both the authenticity and the general integrity of the books of the New Testament may be regarded as finally established."[3]

Conclusion

In summary, the original autographs of the Old and New Testaments are not in the possession of anyone today. However, because of the many copies that exist and the work of biblical historians, we can be confident that today's Bible accurately reflects the inspired writers' work.

Chapter 2

QUESTIONS ABOUT THE PARTS OF THE BIBLE

Contents

Question: Who divided the Bible into chapters and verses? When and why was it done?

Answer: When the books of the Bible were originally written, they did not contain chapter or verse references. The Bible was divided into chapters and verses to help us find particular verses more quickly and easily. It is much easier to find "John chapter 3, verse 16" than it is to find "for God so loved the world ..." Overall, the chapter and verse divisions are very helpful.

In AD 1127, Stephen Langton, Archbishop of Canterbury, developed the chapter divisions commonly used today. The Wycliffe English Bible of 1382 was the first Bible to use this chapter pattern. Since the Wycliffe Bible, nearly all Bible translations have followed Langton's chapter divisions.

A Jewish rabbi named Nathan divided the Old Testament into verses in AD 1448. In 1555, Robert Estienne, also known as Stephanus, became the first to divide the New Testament chapters into verses. Since that time, beginning with the Geneva Bible in 1599, Langston's chapter divisions and Nathan's and Stephanus's verse divisions have been accepted into nearly all the Bible versions.

Question: Old Testament vs. New Testament—what are the differences?

Answer: While the Bible is a unified book, there are differences between the Old Testament and the New Testament. In many ways, they are complementary. The Old Testament is foundational; the New Testament builds on that foundation with further revelation from God. The Old Testament establishes principles that are seen to be illustrative of New Testament truths. The Old Testament contains many prophecies that are fulfilled in the New. The Old Testament provides the history of a *people*; the New Testament focus is on a *Person*. The Old Testament shows the wrath of God against sin (with glimpses of His grace); the New Testament shows the grace of God toward sinners (with glimpses of His wrath).

The Old Testament predicts a Messiah (see Isaiah 53), and the New Testament reveals who the Messiah is (John 4:25–26). The Old

Testament records the giving of God's Law, and the New Testament shows how Jesus the Messiah fulfilled that Law (Matthew 5:17; Hebrews 10:9). In the Old Testament, God's dealings are mainly with His chosen people, the Jews; in the New Testament, God's dealings are mainly with His church (Matthew 16:18). Physical blessings promised under the Old Covenant (Deuteronomy 29:9) give way to spiritual blessings under the New Covenant (Ephesians 1:3).

The Old Testament prophecies related to the coming of Christ, although incredibly detailed, contain a certain amount of ambiguity that is cleared up in the New Testament. For example, the prophet Isaiah spoke of the death of the Messiah (Isaiah 53) and the establishing of the Messiah's kingdom (Isaiah 26), with no clues concerning the chronology of the two events—no hints that the suffering and the kingdom-building might be separated by millennia. In the New Testament, it becomes clear that the Messiah would have *two* advents: in the first He suffered and died (and rose again), and in the second He will establish His kingdom.

Because God's revelation in Scripture is progressive, the New Testament brings into sharper focus principles that were introduced in the Old Testament. The book of Hebrews describes how Jesus is the true High Priest and how His one sacrifice replaces all previous sacrifices, which were mere foreshadowings. The Passover lamb of the Old Testament (Ezra 6:20) becomes the Lamb of God in the New Testament (John 1:29). The Old Testament gives the Law. The New Testament clarifies that the Law was meant to show men their need of salvation and was never intended to be the means of salvation (Romans 3:19).

The Old Testament saw paradise lost for Adam; the New Testament shows how paradise is regained through the second Adam (Christ). The Old Testament declares that man was separated from God through sin (Genesis 3), and the New Testament declares that man can be restored in his relationship to God (Romans 3—6). The Old Testament predicted the Messiah's life. The Gospels record Jesus' life, and the Epistles interpret His life and how we are to respond to all He has done.

In summary, the Old Testament lays the foundation for the coming of the Messiah who would sacrifice Himself for the sins of the world (1 John 2:2). The New Testament records the ministry of Jesus Christ and then looks back on what He did and how we are to respond. Both testaments reveal the same holy, merciful, and righteous God who condemns sin but desires to save sinners through an atoning sacrifice. In both testaments, God reveals Himself to us and shows us how we are to come to Him through faith (Genesis 15:6; Ephesians 2:8).

Question: What is the story of the Old Testament?

Answer: In the very beginning, God was already there. For His own good pleasure, God created time and the universe by the power of His word, turning nothing into something. On the sixth day of creation, God made something unique: mankind—a man and a woman—created in His likeness. As God created the first two humans as male and female, He instituted the covenant of marriage (Genesis 1—2).

God placed the man and his wife in the garden of Eden, a perfect environment, and gave them the responsibility of tending the garden. God allowed them to eat of any fruit in the garden but one: the tree of the knowledge of good and evil was forbidden to them. They had a choice to obey or disobey, but God warned them that death would result if they disobeyed (Genesis 2:15–17).

At some point after the creation week, a mighty angel named Lucifer rebelled against God in heaven. He and one third of the angelic host were cast out of heaven. Lucifer came into the garden where the man and his wife were. There, he took the form of a serpent and tempted Eve, the first woman, to disobey God by eating the forbidden fruit. He told her that she would not die and that the fruit was actually good for her. She believed the lies and ate some of the fruit. She then gave the fruit to her husband, Adam, and he ate it, too. Immediately, the couple knew they had done wrong. They felt ashamed and vulnerable and exposed. When God came looking for them, they hid (Isaiah 14:12–15; Genesis 3:1–13).

Of course, God found them. Judgment was meted out. The ground was cursed for the man's sake—it would no longer bring forth its fruit easily; instead, man must toil to produce a crop. The woman was cursed with pain during childbirth. The serpent was cursed to crawl in the dust from then on. And then God made a promise: one day, Someone would be born who would do battle with the Serpent. This One would crush the Serpent's head, although He would be injured in the process. God then slaughtered an animal and provided coverings of skin for the sinful couple before He drove them out of Eden (Genesis 3:14–19, 21).

The struggle between good and evil continued in the first couple's family. One of their sons, Cain, murdered his brother, Abel, and was cursed for his deed. Another child was born to the first woman. His name was Seth (Genesis 4:8, 25).

Several generations later, the world was filled with wickedness. Violence and a disregard for God were rampant. God determined to destroy the wickedness of man and begin anew. A man named Noah, one of Seth's descendants, was extended grace (God's blessing on the undeserving). God revealed to Noah that He would send a great flood to destroy the earth, and He gave Noah instructions on building an ark to survive the flood. Noah built the ark, and when the time came, God caused animals of each kind to enter the ark. These animals, along with Noah and his family, were spared. The flood destroyed every other non-aquatic creature on the earth (Genesis 6—8).

After the flood, Noah and his family began to repopulate the earth. But when their descendants began building a monument to themselves in defiance of God, God confused their language. The inhabitants of the earth separated according to their language groups and spread out over the face of the earth (Genesis 11:1–8).

The time came for God to begin His plan to introduce the Serpent-crusher into the world. The first step was to create a people set apart for Himself. He chose a man named Abraham and his wife, Sarah, to begin a new race of people. God called Abraham away from his home and led him to the land of Canaan. God promised Abraham innumerable descendants who would possess

Canaan as their own. God also promised to bless Abraham's seed and, through that seed, to bless all the nations of the earth. The problem was that Abraham and Sarah were old, and Sarah was barren. But Abraham believed God's promise, and God reckoned Abraham's faith as righteousness (Genesis 12:1–4; 15:6).

In due time, God blessed Abraham and Sarah with a son, Isaac. God repeated His promise of many descendants and blessing to Isaac. Isaac had twins, Esau and Jacob. God chose Jacob to inherit the promised blessing and changed his name to Israel. Jacob/Israel had twelve sons, who became the heads of the twelve tribes of Israel (Genesis 21:1–6; 25:19–26; 28:10–15; 35:23–26).

Due to a severe famine, Jacob moved his entire family from Canaan to Egypt. Before he died, Jacob gave prophetic blessings to each of his sons. To Judah, he promised there would be a King among his descendants—One who would be honored by all the nations of the world. Jacob's family increased in Egypt, and they remained there for the next 400 years. Then the king of Egypt, fearing that the children of Israel would become too numerous to handle, enslaved them. God raised up a prophet named Moses, from the tribe of Levi, to bring the people of Israel out of Egypt and back to the land God had promised to Abraham (Genesis 46; 49; Exodus 1:8–14; 3:7-10).

The exodus from Egypt was accompanied by many great miracles, including the parting of the Red Sea. Once safely out of Egypt, the children of Israel camped at Mt. Sinai, where God gave Moses the Law. This Law, summarized in the Ten Commandments, was the basis of a covenant God made with Israel: if they kept His commandments, they would be blessed, but if they broke His commandments, they would suffer curses. Israel agreed to follow the Law of God (Exodus 7—11; 14:21–22; 19—20).

In addition to establishing a moral code, the Law defined the role of the priest and prescribed the offering of sacrifices to atone for sin. Atonement could only be made by the shedding of the blood of a spotless sacrifice. The Law also detailed how to build the holy tabernacle, or tent, in which God's presence would dwell and where He would meet with His people (Leviticus 1; Exodus 25:8–9).

After receiving the Law, Moses led the Israelites to the border of the Promised Land. But the people, fearing Canaan's warlike inhabitants and doubting God's promises, refused to enter. As a punishment, God turned them back into the wilderness, where they were forced to wander for 40 years. In His grace, God miraculously provided food and water for the entire multitude (Numbers 14:1–4, 34–35; Exodus 16:35).

At the end of the 40 years of wandering, Moses died. One of his last prophecies concerned the coming of another Prophet who would be like Moses and to whom the people must listen. Moses' successor, Joshua, was used by God to lead the people of Israel into the Promised Land. They went with God's promise that none of their enemies would be able to stand against them. God showed His power at Jericho, the first city they encountered, by causing the walls of the city to fall down flat. In His grace and mercy, God spared a believing prostitute named Rahab from Jericho's destruction (Deuteronomy 18:15; Joshua 6).

Over the next years, Joshua and the Israelites succeeded in driving out most of the Canaanites, and the land was divided among the twelve tribes. However, the conquest of the land was incomplete. Through a lack of faith and simple disobedience, they failed to finish the job, and pockets of Canaanites remained. These pagan influences had an effect on the Israelites, who began to adopt the worship of idols, in direct violation of God's Law (Joshua 15:63; 16:10; 18:1).

After Joshua's death, the Israelites experienced a tumultuous time. The nation would lapse into idolatry, and God would bring judgment in the form of enslavement to an enemy. The people of God would repent and call on the Lord for help. God would then raise up a judge to destroy the idols, rally the people, and defeat the enemy. Peace would last for a while, but, after the death of the judge, the people invariably fell back into idolatry, and the cycle would repeat (Judges 17:6).

The final judge was Samuel, who was also a prophet. During his time, Israel demanded a king to rule over them, in order to be like the other nations. God granted their request, and Samuel anointed

Saul as Israel's first king. Saul was a disappointment, however. He disobeyed God and was removed from power. God chose David, of the tribe of Judah, to succeed Saul as king. God promised David that he would have a descendant who would reign on the throne forever (1 Samuel 8:5; 15:1, 26; 1 Chronicles 17:11–14).

David's son Solomon reigned in Jerusalem after David's death. During the reign of Solomon's son, civil war broke out, and the kingdom was divided: the northern kingdom was called Israel, and the southern kingdom was called Judah. The Davidic dynasty ruled in Judah (1 Kings 2:1, 12).

The northern kingdom of Israel had an unbroken series of wicked kings. None of them sought the Lord or attempted to lead the nation according to God's Law. God sent prophets to warn them, including the miracle-working Elijah and Elisha, but the kings persisted in their wickedness. Finally, God brought the Assyrian nation upon Israel in judgment. The Assyrians deported most of the Israelites, and that was the end of the northern kingdom (1 Kings 17:1; 2 Kings 2; 17).

The southern kingdom of Judah had its share of wicked kings, but the chain was broken by an occasional godly king who truly loved the Lord and sought to govern according to the Law. God was faithful to His promise and blessed the people when they followed His commandments. The nation was preserved during the Assyrian invasion and endured many other threats. During this time, the prophet Isaiah preached against the sins of Judah and foresaw the Babylonian invasion. Isaiah also predicted the coming of the Servant of the Lord—one who would suffer for the sins of His people and be glorified and sit on David's throne. The prophet Micah predicted that the Promised One would be born in Bethlehem (Isaiah 37; 53:5; Micah 5:2).

Eventually, the nation of Judah also fell into gross idolatry. God brought the nation of Babylon against Judah in judgment. The prophet Jeremiah experienced the fall of Jerusalem and predicted that the Jewish captives in Babylon would return to the Promised Land after 70 years. Jeremiah also prophesied a future covenant in which the Law was not written on tablets of stone but in the hearts of God's people. This new covenant would result in God's forgiveness of sin (2 Kings 25:8–10; Jeremiah 29:10; 31:31–34).

As prophesied, the Babylon captivity lasted for 70 years. The prophets Daniel and Ezekiel ministered during that time. Daniel predicted the rise and fall of many nations. He also predicted the coming of the Messiah, or Chosen One, who would be killed for the sake of others (Daniel 2:36–45; 9:26).

After Babylon fell to the Persians, the Jews were released to return to Judah. Many Jews returned home to rebuild Jerusalem and the temple. Nehemiah and Ezra led those endeavors, with encouragement from the prophets Haggai and Zechariah. One of Zechariah's prophecies included a description of a future King who would come into Jerusalem humbly, riding on a donkey (Nehemiah 6:15–16; Ezra 6:14–15; Zechariah 9:9).

Not all of the Jews returned to Judah, however. Many chose to stay in Persia, where God still watched over them. A Jewess named Esther rose to the rank of queen of Persia and was instrumental in saving the lives of all the Jews in the kingdom (Esther 8:1).

Malachi wrote the last book of the Old Testament. He prophesied that the Lord would come to His temple, but, before His arrival, another messenger would prepare the way for the Lord. This messenger would be like the prophet Elijah of old. After Malachi's prophecy, it was another 400 years before God spoke directly to man (Malachi 3:1; 4:5).

The Old Testament is the story of God's plan to bring about the redemption of man. At the close of the Old Testament, God has a unique Chosen People who understand the importance of blood sacrifices, who believe the promises made to Abraham and David, and who are awaiting a Redeemer. In short, they are ready to receive the Serpent-crusher of Genesis, the Prophet like Moses, the Suffering Servant of Isaiah, the Son of David, the Messiah of Daniel, and the Humble King of Zechariah—all to be found in one person, Jesus Christ.

Question: What is the story of the New Testament?

Answer: Four hundred years after God spoke to the prophet Malachi, God spoke again. The message was that the prophecy of Malachi 3:1 was soon to be fulfilled, that a prophet was to prepare the way for the Lord. The Messiah was on His way.

That prophet was named John. The Messiah was named Jesus, born to a virgin named Mary. Jesus grew up as an observant Jew. When He was about thirty years old, He began His public ministry to Israel. John had been preaching of the coming Messianic Kingdom and baptizing those who believed his message and repented of their sins. When Jesus came to be baptized, God spoke audibly, and the Holy Spirit came visibly upon Jesus, identifying Him as the promised Messiah. From that time on, John's ministry waned, having fulfilled its purpose of introducing Christ to the world (Matthew 3).

Jesus called twelve disciples from various walks of life, empowered them for service, and began training them. As Jesus traveled and preached, He healed the sick and performed many other miracles that authenticated His message. Jesus' early ministry saw tremendous growth. Vast crowds, awed by the miracles and amazed at His teaching, followed Him wherever He went (Luke 9:1; Matthew 19:2).

Not everyone was enthralled by Jesus, however. The political and religious leaders of the Jewish community took offense to Jesus' teaching that their rules and traditions were not the path to salvation. They confronted Jesus many times, and Jesus openly spoke of them as hypocrites. The Pharisees observed Jesus' miracles but attributed them to the work of the devil rather than giving God the glory (Matthew 12:24; 15:3; Matthew 23).

The crowds who followed Jesus grew sparser as it became apparent that Jesus had no intention of making Himself a king or of overthrowing the Roman oppressors. John was arrested and eventually executed in prison. Jesus began to focus more on His twelve disciples, most of whom acknowledged that He was the Son of God. Only one did not believe; his name was Judas, and he actively began to seek a way to betray Jesus to the authorities (John 6:66; Matthew 16:16; 26:16).

In His final trip to Jerusalem, Jesus celebrated Passover with His disciples. That night, during a time of prayer, Judas led an armed mob to Jesus. Jesus was arrested and dragged through a series of mock trials. He was condemned to death by crucifixion by the Roman governor, who nevertheless admitted that Jesus was an innocent man. Jesus was crucified. At the moment of His death, there was a great earthquake. Jesus' dead body was taken from the cross and hurriedly laid in a nearby tomb (Luke 22:14–23, 39–53; Mark 15:15, 25; Matthew 27:51; John 19:42).

On the third day after Jesus' death, Jesus' tomb was discovered empty, and angels announced that He had risen. Jesus then appeared in the flesh to His disciples and spent time with them during the next forty days. At the end of that time, Jesus commissioned the apostles and ascended into heaven as they watched (Luke 24:6; John 21:1, 14; Acts 1:3–9).

Ten days after Jesus' ascension to heaven, about 120 disciples were gathered in Jerusalem, praying and waiting for the Holy Spirit, who had been promised by Jesus. On the Day of Pentecost, the Spirit filled the disciples, giving them the ability to speak in languages they had never learned. Peter and the others preached in the streets of Jerusalem, and that day 3,000 people believed the message that the Lord Jesus had died and risen again. Those who believed were baptized in Jesus' name. The church had begun (Acts 2).

The Jerusalem church continued to grow as the apostles performed miracles and taught with great power. However, the new believers soon faced persecution, spearheaded by a young Pharisee named Saul. Many believers had to leave Jerusalem, and, as they went, they spread the good news of Jesus to other cities. Gatherings of believers began to spring up in other communities (Acts 2:43; 8:1, 4).

One of the places that received the gospel was Samaria. The Jerusalem church sent Peter and John to Samaria to verify the reports they had heard concerning a church there. When Peter and John arrived, they witnessed the coming of the Holy Spirit on the

Samaritans in the same way that He had come upon them. Without a doubt, the church had spread to Samaria. Soon thereafter, Peter witnessed the Holy Spirit's coming on a Roman centurion and his household; thus, the church was spreading to the Gentile world as well (Acts 8:14–17; 10:27–48).

James, one of the twelve disciples, was martyred in Jerusalem. Saul had plans to take his hatred of Christians to Damascus, but on the way Jesus appeared to him in a vision. The former persecutor of the church was transformed into an ardent preacher of Christ. A few years later, Saul (now known as Paul) became a teacher in the church in Antioch. While there, he and Barnabas were chosen by the Holy Spirit to become the world's first "foreign missionaries," and they left for Cyprus and Asia Minor. Paul and Barnabas suffered much persecution and difficulty on their journey, but many people were saved—including a young man named Timothy—and churches were established (Acts 9:1–22; 12:1–2; Acts 13—14).

Back in Jerusalem, a question arose over the acceptance of Gentiles into the church. Were Gentile Christians (former pagans) to be given equal standing as Jewish Christians, who had kept the Law all their lives? More specifically, did Gentile believers have to be circumcised in order to be saved? A council met in Jerusalem to consider this question. Peter and Paul both gave testimony of how God had granted the Holy Spirit to the Gentile believers without the rite of circumcision. The council's determination was that salvation is by grace through faith and that circumcision was not necessary for salvation (Acts 15:1–31).

Paul went on another missionary journey, accompanied this time by Silas. Along the way, Timothy joined them, as did a doctor named Luke. At the behest of the Holy Spirit, Paul and company left Asia Minor and traveled to Greece, where even more churches were established in Philippi, Thessalonica, Corinth, Ephesus, and other cities. Later, Paul went on a third missionary journey. His modus operandi was almost always the same—preach in a city's synagogue first, presenting the gospel to the Jews in each community. Usually, he was rejected in the synagogues, and he would take the message to the Gentiles instead (Acts 15:40—21:17).

Against the warnings of friends, Paul made a trip to Jerusalem. There, he was attacked by a mob intent on killing him. He was rescued by a Roman tribune and kept in protective custody in the barracks. Paul stood trial before the Sanhedrin in Jerusalem, but the court erupted in chaos, and Paul was taken to Caesarea to stand trial before a Roman judge. After several years in Caesarea, Paul appealed to Caesar, as was his right under Roman law (Acts 21:12, 27–36; Acts 23:1–25:12).

Paul was taken to Rome as a prisoner on a ship, and Luke accompanied him. On the way, a severe storm wrecked the ship, but everyone aboard made it safely to the island of Malta. There, Paul performed miracles that caught the attention of the governor of the island. Again, the gospel spread (Acts 27:1–28:10).

When he arrived in Rome, Paul was put under house arrest. His friends could visit, and he had a certain amount of freedom to teach. Some of the Roman guards were converted, and even some of Caesar's own household believed in Jesus (Acts 28:16, 30–31; Philippians 4:22).

While Paul was being held in Rome, the work of God continued around the Mediterranean world. Timothy ministered in Ephesus; Titus oversaw the work in Crete; Apollos served in Corinth; Peter, possibly, went to Rome (1 Timothy 1:3; Titus 1:5; Acts 19:1; 1 Peter 5:13).

Most of the apostles were martyred for their faith in Christ. The last apostle was John who, as an old man, was exiled to the island of Patmos. There, he received from the Lord Jesus messages for the churches and a vision of the end times that he recorded as the book of Revelation (Revelation 1:9, 4, 19).

Question: What are the Synoptic Gospels?

Answer: The Synoptic Gospels are the first three books of the New Testament—Matthew, Mark, and Luke. These three books plus John are called the "Gospels" because they chronicle the good news of Jesus' life, death, and resurrection—the basis of our salvation. Matthew, one of the twelve apostles commissioned by Jesus, wrote the gospel of Matthew. John Mark, a close associate of the apostle Peter, wrote the gospel of Mark. Luke the physician, a friend and traveling companion of the apostle Paul, wrote the gospel of Luke.

The first three gospels are called "synoptic" because they "see together with a common view" (the word *synoptic* literally means "together sight"). Matthew, Mark, and Luke cover many of the same events in Jesus' life—most of them from Jesus' ministry in Galilee—in much the same order. Nearly 90 percent of Mark's content is found in Matthew, and about 50 percent of Mark's content appears in Luke. All of the parables of Christ are found in the Synoptics (the gospel of John contains no parables).

There are differences, too. Matthew and Luke are both considerably longer than Mark. Matthew was written for a Jewish audience, Mark for a Roman audience, and Luke for a broader Gentile audience. Matthew quotes extensively from the Old Testament, and his oft use (32 times) of the phrase "the kingdom of heaven" is unique—it is not found anywhere else in the Bible. Luke places a definite emphasis on Jesus' acts of compassion toward Gentiles and Samaritans. Much of Luke 10—20 is unique to that gospel.

The difficulty in explaining the similarities and differences among the Synoptic Gospels is referred to as the Synoptic Problem in the world of biblical scholarship. In the final analysis, the Synoptic "Problem" is not much of a problem at all—God inspired three gospel writers to record the events surrounding the same Person during the same part of His life in the same locations, yet with slightly different emphases aimed at different readers.

Question: Why did God give us four gospels?

Answer: Here are some reasons why God gave four gospels instead of just one:

1) **To give a more complete picture of Christ.** While the entire Bible is inspired by God (2 Timothy 3:16), He used human authors with different backgrounds and personalities to accomplish His

purposes through their writing. Each of the gospel authors had a distinct objective behind his gospel, and in carrying out those objectives, each emphasized different aspects of the person and ministry of Jesus Christ.

Matthew was writing to a Hebrew audience, and one of his intents was to show from Jesus' genealogy and fulfillment of Old Testament prophecies that He was the long-expected Messiah, and thus should be believed in. Matthew's emphasis is that Jesus is the promised King, the "Son of David," who would forever sit upon the throne of Israel (Matthew 9:27; 21:9).

Mark was an eyewitness to the events in the life of Christ as well as a friend of the apostle Peter. Mark wrote for a Gentile audience, as we see by his exclusion of things important to Jewish readers (genealogies, Christ's controversies with Jewish leaders of His day, frequent references to the Old Testament, etc.). Mark emphasizes Christ as the suffering Servant, the One who came "not to be served, but to serve, and to give His life as a ransom for many" (Mark 10:45).

Luke, the "beloved physician" (Colossians 4:14 KJV), evangelist, and companion of the apostle Paul, wrote both the gospel of Luke and the Acts of the Apostles. Luke is the only Gentile author of the New Testament. Those who have used his writings in genealogical and historical studies have long accepted him as a diligent master historian. As a historian, he states that it is his intent to write down an orderly account of the life of Christ based on the reports of those who were eyewitnesses (Luke 1:1–4). Because Luke specifically wrote for the benefit of Theophilus (apparently a Gentile of some stature), his gospel was composed with a Gentile audience in mind, and his intent was to show that a Christian's faith is based upon historically reliable and verifiable events. Luke often refers to Christ as the "Son of Man," emphasizing His humanity, and he shares many details that are not found in the other gospel accounts.

The gospel of John, written by John the apostle, is distinct from the other three gospels and contains much theological content in regard to the person of Christ and the meaning of faith. Matthew,

Mark, and Luke are referred to as the "Synoptic Gospels" because of their similar styles and content in giving a synopsis of the life of Christ. The gospel of John begins not with Jesus' birth or earthly ministry, but with the activity and characteristics of the Son of God before He became man (John 1:1–14). The gospel of John emphasizes the deity of Christ, as is seen in his use of such phrases as "the Word was God" (John 1:1), "the Savior of the world" (John 4:42), the "Son of God" (used repeatedly), and "Lord and ... God" (John 20:28). Jesus also affirms His deity in John's gospel with several "I Am" statements; most notable among them is John 8:58, in which He states that "before Abraham was born, I am!" (compare to Exodus 3:13–14). But John also emphasizes the fact of Jesus' humanity, desiring to correct the error of the Gnostics, who did not believe in Christ's humanity. John's gospel spells out his overall purpose for writing: "Jesus did many other miraculous signs in the presence of his disciples, which are not recorded in this book. But these are written that you may believe that Jesus is the Christ, the Son of God, and that by believing you may have life in his name" (John 20:30–31).

The four distinct and yet equally accurate accounts of Christ reveal different aspects of His person and ministry. Each account becomes like a different-colored thread in a tapestry woven to form a more complete picture of this One who is beyond description. And while we will never fully understand everything about Jesus Christ (John 20:30), through the four Gospels we can know enough of Him to appreciate who He is and what He has done for us so that we may have life through faith in Him.

2) **To enable us to objectively verify the truthfulness of their accounts.** The Bible, from earliest times, states that judgment in a court of law was not to be made against a person based on the testimony of a single eyewitness but that a minimum of two or three was required (Deuteronomy 19:15). Having different accounts of the person and earthly ministry of Jesus Christ enables us to assess the accuracy of the information we have concerning Him.

Simon Greenleaf, a well-known and accepted authority on what constitutes reliable evidence in a court of law, examined the four gospels from a legal perspective. He noted that the type of eyewitness accounts given in the four Gospels—accounts which agree, but with each writer choosing to omit or add details different from the others—is typical of reliable, independent sources that would be accepted in a court of law as strong evidence. Had the Gospels contained exactly the same information with the same details written from the same perspective, it would indicate collusion—the writers getting together beforehand to "get their stories straight" in order to make their writings seem credible. The differences among the Gospels, even the apparent contradictions of details upon first examination, speak to the independent nature of the writings. Thus, the independent nature of the four gospel accounts—agreeing in their information but differing in perspective, amount of detail, and which events were recorded—indicate that the record of Christ's life and ministry is factual and reliable.

3) **To reward those who are diligent seekers.** Much can be gained by an individual study of each of the Gospels. But still more can be gained by comparing and contrasting the different accounts of specific events during Jesus' ministry. For instance, Matthew 14 gives the account of the feeding of the 5,000 and Jesus walking on the water. In Matthew 14:22, we are told, "Jesus made the disciples get into the boat and go on ahead of him to the other side, while he dismissed the crowd." Why did He do this? There is no apparent reason given in Matthew's account. But when we combine it with the account in Mark 6, we see that the disciples had come back from casting out demons and healing people through the authority Jesus had given them when He sent them out two-by-two (Mark 6:7–13). But they returned with "big heads," forgetting their place and ready now to instruct Him (Matthew 14:15). So, in sending them off in the evening to go to the other side of the Sea of Galilee, Jesus reveals two things to them. As they struggle against the wind and waves in their own self-reliance until the early hours of the morning (Mark 6:48), they begin to see that 1) they can achieve nothing for God in their own ability and 2) nothing is impossible if they call upon Him and live in dependence upon His power. There are many passages containing similar "jewels" to be found

by the diligent student of the Word of God who takes the time to compare Scripture with Scripture.

Question: What is the harmony of the Gospels?

Answer: The "harmony" of the Gospels is the agreement of the four biblical Gospels. The four New Testament Gospels are like the singers in a four-part choir. They each have a distinct part to sing, yet the parts combine to make a beautiful composition. Each of the four Gospels gives testimony of Jesus from a slightly different perspective, but they all tell the same story. Thus, they are all in harmony with one another. Books that align the gospel accounts chronologically are called harmonies of the Gospels, and some Bibles include a reference section called a "Harmony of the Gospels," doing the same thing.

Matthew, Mark, and Luke are called the "Synoptic Gospels" because they include many of the same events from the life of Jesus (the word *synoptic* means "same view"). John stands on its own, filling in gaps that the others leave out. Each one of these gospels was written for a different audience and emphasizes different facets of Jesus' ministry. The gospel of Matthew was written primarily for the Jews and emphasizes how Jesus fulfilled the prophecies of a kingly Messiah. Mark was written primarily for Roman or Gentile Christians, so it includes few Old Testament prophecies and explains many Jewish words and customs. Jesus is portrayed in Mark as the Divine Servant. Luke was also written primarily for Gentile believers, so it also explains Jewish customs and uses Greek names. Luke set out to write an orderly narrative of the life of Jesus and presents Jesus as the Son of Man, emphasizing His full humanity. John's gospel emphasizes Jesus as the Son of God and includes more of Jesus' revelations about Himself than any of the other gospels. It also gives a much more detailed picture of the events during Jesus' last days.

Some people have attempted to discredit the Bible by pointing out seeming inconsistencies in the gospel narratives. They point out differences in the order in which events are presented or minor details within those events. When the four accounts are placed side by side, we see that they do not all follow the same strict chronology. This is because much of the narrative is arranged in topical order, in which events are grouped according to similar theme. This topical approach is the way most of us carry on conversations every day.

Differences in minor details, such as the number of angels at Christ's tomb (Matthew 28:5; Mark 16:5; Luke 24:4; John 20:12), are also answered by allowing the text to speak for itself. Matthew and Mark mention "an angel," while Luke and John mention two angels. However, Matthew and Mark never say there was "only" one angel; they simply say there was an angel present. Such differences are complementary, not contradictory. New information may be added, but it never negates the veracity of the old information.

Like the rest of Scripture, the four Gospels are a beautiful testimony of God's revelation to man. Imagine a tax collector (Matthew), an untrained Jewish lad with a history as a quitter (Mark), a Roman doctor (Luke), and a Jewish fisherman (John) all writing harmonious testimonies of the life of Jesus. There is no way, without God's intervention, that they could have written these amazingly accurate accounts (2 Timothy 3:16). The history, the prophecy, and the personal details all work together to compose one supremely accurate picture of Jesus—the Messiah, the King, the Servant, and the Son of God.

Question: What is the Pentateuch?

Answer: The Pentateuch is a name for the first five books of the Bible. Even though the books of the Pentateuch themselves do not expressly identify the author, there are many passages that attribute them to Moses or as being his words (Exodus 17:14; 24:4–7; Numbers 33:1–2; Deuteronomy 31:9–13; 24–26). One of the most important evidences for Moses being the author of the Pentateuch is that Jesus Himself refers to this section of the Old Testament as the "Law of Moses" (Luke 24:44). While there are some verses in the Pentateuch which appear to have been added by someone other than Moses—for example, Deuteronomy 34:5–8, which describes the death and burial of Moses—most scholars attribute the majority of these books to Moses. Even if Joshua or someone else acted as a scribe for the original manuscripts, the teaching and revelation can be traced from God through Moses.

The word *Pentateuch* comes from a combination of the Greek word *penta*, meaning "five," and *teuchos*, which can be translated "scroll." Therefore, *Pentateuch* simply refers to the five scrolls that comprise the first of three divisions of the Jewish canon. The name can be traced as far back as AD 200, when Tertullian referred to the first five books of the Bible as the Pentateuch. Also known as the Torah, which is the Hebrew word meaning "Law," these five books of the Bible are Genesis, Exodus, Leviticus, Numbers, and Deuteronomy.

Jews generally have divided the Old Testament into three sections: The Law, The Prophets, and The Writings. The Law or Torah contains the historical background of creation and God's choosing of Abraham and the Jewish nation. The Torah also contains the Law given to Israel at Mount Sinai. Scripture refers to these five books by various names. In Joshua 1:7, they are said to be the "law (Torah) my servant Moses gave to you," and they are called "the law of Moses" in 1 Kings 2:3.

The five books of the Bible that make up the Pentateuch are the beginning of God's progressive revelation to man. In Genesis we find the creation, the fall of man, the promise of redemption, the beginning of human civilization, and the establishment of God's covenant relationship with His chosen nation, Israel.

The next book is Exodus, which records God's deliverance of His covenant people from slavery in Egypt and their preparation for possessing the Promised Land that God had set aside for them. Exodus also details the covenant God made with Israel at Mount Sinai, the instructions for building the tabernacle, the giving of the Ten Commandments, and other instructions on how Israel was to worship God.

Leviticus follows Exodus and expands on the instructions for how Israel was to worship God and govern themselves. Leviticus lays out the requirements of the sacrificial system that would allow

God to overlook the sins of His people until the perfect sacrifice of Christ, whose death completely atoned for sin.

Following Leviticus is Numbers, which covers key events during the 40 years of Israel's wandering in the wilderness and gives instructions for worshiping God and living as His covenant people.

The last of the five books that comprise the Pentateuch is Deuteronomy. Deuteronomy is sometimes referred to as the "second law" or "repetition of the law" (the word *Deuteronomy* literally means "second law"). The book records the final words of Moses before the people of Israel entered the Promised Land (Deuteronomy 1:1). In Deuteronomy God's Law given at Mount Sinai is repeated for a new generation of Jacob's children. As Israel entered a new chapter of their history, Moses reminds them of God's commandments and promise of blessings for obedience and curses for disobedience.

While five books of the Pentateuch are often called the Torah or the Law, in reality they contain much more than laws. They provide a foreshadowing of God's plan of redemption and create a backdrop for everything that follows in Scripture. Like the rest of the Old Testament, the promises, types, and prophecies contained in the Pentateuch have their ultimate fulfillment in the person and work of Jesus Christ.

Chapter 3

QUESTIONS ABOUT THE
BIBLICAL CANON

Contents

Question: What is the canon of Scripture?

Answer: The word *canon* comes from the rule of law that was used to determine if a book measured up to a standard. It is important to note that the writings of Scripture were canonical at the moment they were written. Scripture was Scripture when the pen touched the parchment. This is very important because Christianity does not start by defining God or Jesus Christ or salvation. The basis of Christianity is found in the authority of Scripture. If we cannot identify what Scripture is, then we cannot properly distinguish any theological truth from error.

What measure or standard was used to determine which books should be classified as Scripture? A key verse in understanding the process and purpose, and perhaps the timing of the giving of Scripture, is Jude 3, which states that a Christian's faith "was once for all entrusted to the saints." Since our faith is defined by Scripture, Jude is essentially saying that Scripture was given once for the benefit of all Christians. Isn't it wonderful to know that there are no hidden or lost manuscripts yet to be found, there are no secret books only familiar to a select few, and there are no people alive who have special revelation requiring us to trek up a Himalayan mountain in order to be enlightened? We can be confident that God has not left us without a witness. The same supernatural power God used to produce His Word has also preserved it.

Psalm 119:160 states that the entirety of God's Word is truth. Starting with that premise, we can compare writings outside the accepted canon of Scripture to see if they meet the test. As an example, the Bible claims that Jesus Christ is God (Isaiah 9:6–7; Matthew 1:22–23; John 1:1, 14; 20:28; Philippians 2:5–6; Colossians 2:9; Titus 2:13; Hebrews 1:8). Yet many extra-biblical texts, claiming to be Scripture, argue that Jesus is not God. When clear contradictions exist, the established Bible is to be trusted, leaving the others outside the sphere of Scripture.

In the early centuries of the church, Christians were sometimes put to death for possessing copies of Scripture. Because of this persecution, the question soon came up: "What books are worth dying for?" Some books may have contained sayings of Jesus, but were they inspired as stated in 2 Timothy 3:16? Church councils played a role in publicly recognizing the canon of Scripture, but often an individual church or groups of churches recognized a book as inspired from the time of its writing (e.g., Colossians 4:16; 1 Thessalonians 5:27). Throughout the early centuries of the church, few books were ever disputed, and the list was basically settled by AD 303.

When it came to the Old Testament, three important facts were considered: 1) the New Testament quotes from or alludes to every Old Testament book but two; 2) Jesus effectively endorsed the Hebrew canon in Matthew 23:35 when He cited one of the first narratives and one of the last in the Scriptures of His day; 3) the Jews were meticulous in preserving the Old Testament Scriptures, and they had few controversies over what parts belonged or did not belong. The Roman Catholic Apocrypha did not measure up and has never been accepted by the Jews as Scripture.

Most questions about which books belong in the Bible dealt with writings from the time of Christ forward. The early church had some specific criteria for books to meet in order be considered as part of the New Testament. Was the book written by someone who was an eyewitness of Jesus Christ? Did the book pass the "truth test"—i.e., did it concur with other, already agreed-upon Scripture? The New Testament books they accepted back then have endured the test of time, and Christian orthodoxy has embraced these, with little challenge, for centuries.

Confidence in the acceptance of specific books dates back to the first-century recipients who offered firsthand testimony as to their authenticity. Furthermore, the end-time subject matter of the book of Revelation, and the prohibition against adding to the words of the final book (Revelation 22:18), argue that the canon was closed when John finished writing (c. AD 95).

There is an important theological point that should not be missed. God has used His word for millennia for one primary purpose—to reveal Himself and communicate to mankind. Ultimately, the church councils did not decide if a book was

Scripture; that was decided when God chose the human author to write His words. In order to preserve His Word through the centuries, God guided the early church councils in their recognition of the canon.

The knowledge of such things as the true nature of God, the origin of the universe and life, the purpose and meaning of life, the wonders of salvation, and future events (including the destiny of mankind) is beyond the natural observational and scientific capacity of mankind. The once-delivered Word of God, valued and personally applied by Christians for centuries, is sufficient to explain to us everything we need to know of Christ (Acts 18:28; Galatians 3:22; 2 Timothy 3:15) and to teach us, correct us, and instruct us in all righteousness (2 Timothy 3:16).

Question: How and when was the canon of the Bible put together?

Answer: The term *canon* is used to describe the books that are divinely inspired and therefore belong in the Bible. The difficulty in determining the biblical canon is that the Bible does not give us a list of the books that belong in the Bible. Determining the canon was a process conducted first by Jewish rabbis and scholars and later by early Christians. Ultimately, it was God who decided what books belonged in the biblical canon. A book of Scripture belonged in the canon from the moment God inspired its writing. It was simply a matter of God's convincing His human followers which books should be included in the Bible.

Compared to the New Testament, there was very little controversy over the canon of the Old Testament. Hebrew believers recognized God's messengers and accepted their writings as inspired of God. While there was undeniably some debate in regard to the Old Testament canon, by AD 250 there was nearly universal agreement on the canon of Hebrew Scripture. The only issue that remained was the Apocrypha, with some debate and discussion continuing today. The vast majority of Hebrew scholars considered the Apocrypha to be good historical and religious documents, but not on the same level as the Hebrew Scriptures.

For the New Testament, the process of the recognition and collection began in the first centuries of the Christian church. Very early on, some of the New Testament books were being recognized. Paul considered Luke's writings to be as authoritative as the Old Testament (1 Timothy 5:18; compare to Deuteronomy 25:4 and Luke 10:7). Peter recognized Paul's writings as Scripture (2 Peter 3:15–16). Some of the books of the New Testament were being circulated among the churches (Colossians 4:16; 1 Thessalonians 5:27). Clement of Rome mentioned at least eight New Testament books (AD 95). Ignatius of Antioch acknowledged about seven books (AD 115). Polycarp, a disciple of John the apostle, acknowledged 15 books (AD 108). Later, Irenaeus mentioned 21 books (AD 185). Hippolytus recognized 22 books (ad 170–235). The New Testament books books over which there was the most controversy were Hebrews, James, 2 Peter, 2 John, and 3 John.

The first "canon" was the Muratorian Canon, which was compiled in AD 170. The Muratorian Canon included all of the New Testament books except Hebrews, James, and 3 John. In AD 363, the Council of Laodicea stated that only the Old Testament (along with the Apocrypha) and the 27 books of the New Testament were to be read in the churches. The Council of Hippo (AD 393) and the Council of Carthage (AD 397) also affirmed the same 27 books as authoritative.

The councils followed something similar to the following principles to determine whether a New Testament book was truly inspired by the Holy Spirit: 1) Was the author an apostle or did he have a close connection with an apostle? 2) Is the book accepted by the body of Christ at large? 3) Did the book contain consistency of doctrine and orthodox teaching? 4) Did the book bear evidence of high moral and spiritual values that would reflect a work of the Holy Spirit? If the answer to these four questions was yes, then the book was recognized as canonical. Again, it is crucial to remember that the church did not determine the canon. No early church council decided on the canon. It was God, and God alone, who determined which books belonged in the Bible. It was simply a matter of God's imparting to His followers what He had already decided. The human process of collecting the books of the Bible was flawed, but God, in His sovereignty, and despite our ignorance and stubbornness, brought the early church to the recognition of the books He had inspired.

Question: How do we decide which books belong in the Bible since the Bible does not say which books to include?

Answer: If Scripture is to be our sole authority, on what authority do we know which books belong in the Bible—since the Bible does not state which books should be in the Bible? This is a very important question, because a chain is only as strong as its weakest link. In the chain of communication from God to humanity, is there a weak link? If so, then the whole chain fails, and the communication ultimately cannot be trusted.

Consider the various "links" comprising God's communication to us: first came God's desire to communicate. This was rooted in His love, for the most loving thing a good God can do is reveal Himself to His creation. Next came the actual transmission of God's Word through human writers. This involved a process the Bible calls "inspiration," in which God breathed the words the human agents recorded (2 Timothy 3:16). After that came dissemination, as the Word was delivered to its audience through preaching or other means. Then came recognition, as God's people distinguished Holy Scripture from other religious writings. And then, preservation, through which God's Word has survived to the present day, despite many attempts to destroy it. And finally, illumination, as the Holy Spirit opens the believer's understanding to receive the Word.

And that's the "chain"—the demonstration of God's love in the inspiration, dissemination, recognition, preservation, and illumination of His Word. We believe that God was involved in each step of the process, for why would God go to such lengths to inspire His Word and then not preserve it? Why would He speak to us and then fail to guide us in recognizing His speech?

This recognition of God's Word is usually called "canonization." We are careful to say that God determined the canon, and the church discovered the canon. The church did not create the canon of Scripture; rather, the church discovered or recognized it. In other words, God's Word was inspired and authoritative from its inception—it "stands firm in the heavens" (Psalm 119:89)—and the church simply recognized that fact and accepted it.

The criteria the church used for recognizing and collecting the Word of God are as follows:

1. Was the book written by a prophet of God? Did the book receive apostolic approval?
2. Was the writer authenticated by miracles to confirm his message?
3. Does the book tell the truth about God, with no falsehood or contradiction?
4. Does the book demonstrate a divine capacity to transform lives?
5. Was the book accepted as God's Word by the people to whom it was first delivered?

Of these criteria, the first one is most important—was the book written by a prophet? Its corollary, "Did the book receive apostolic approval?", was the chief test of canonicity in the early church. This criterion is a logical result of knowing what an "apostle" was. The apostles were gifted by God to be the founders and leaders of the church, so it is reasonable to accept that through them came the Word governing the church.

The apostles were promised the Spirit of truth who would bring to their remembrance what Christ had said (John 14:26) and guide them into "all truth" (John 16:13). After the ascension of Christ, the apostles received supernatural gifts to enable their work and confirm their message (Acts 2:4). God's household is "built on the foundation of the apostles and prophets" (Ephesians 2:20). Given the apostles' special commission, it only makes sense that the church made apostolicity the primary test of canonicity. Thus, the gospel of Matthew was considered canonical (it was written by an apostle); and the gospel of Mark, with its close association with the apostle Peter, was also accepted.

When the New Testament was being written, the individual books and letters were immediately accepted as God's Word and circulated for the benefits of others. The church of Thessalonica received Paul's word as the Word of God (1 Thessalonians 2:13). Paul's epistles were authoritative (2 Thessalonians 3:14) and to be read "to all the brothers [and sisters]" (1 Thessalonians 5:27). Peter recognized Paul's writings as inspired by God and equated them with "the rest of the Scriptures" (2 Peter 3:15–16). Paul quoted the gospel of Luke and called it "Scripture" (1 Timothy 5:18). This widespread acceptance stands in stark contrast to the few debated books, eventually rejected as non-canonical, that enjoyed a limited favor for a time.

Later, as heresy increased and some within the church began clamoring for the acceptance of spurious religious writings, the church wisely held a council to officially confirm their acceptance of the 27 New Testament books. The criteria they used allowed them to objectively distinguish what God had given from that of human origin. They concluded that they would stay with the books that were universally accepted. In so doing, they determined to continue in "the apostles' teaching" (Acts 2:42).

Question: Why isn't the Bible in chronological order?

Answer: The books of the Bible are primarily divided by the type of literature they represent. The books of Genesis through Esther are mostly historical, Job through Song of Solomon are poetry, and Isaiah through Malachi are prophecy. Similarly, the New Testament books of Matthew through Acts are historical, Romans through Jude are letters to churches or individuals, and Revelation is prophecy.

The fact that the Bible is not in chronological order can sometimes make studying the Bible difficult. That is when a chronological Bible can come in handy. In a chronological Bible, each book is placed in order according to the timeline of events it describes. As an example, Isaiah's prophecies are placed in the appropriate places within the books of 1 and 2 Kings, because Isaiah ministered during the times of the kings. Something similar is done in the New Testament, with some of the Epistles being placed within the book of Acts.

Whether or not you choose to utilize a chronological Bible, God's Word should be read and studied. While it is beneficial to understand the chronological events of Scripture, it is most important to study and apply the message of God's Word.

Question: Is it possible that more books could be added to the Bible?

Answer: There is no reason to believe that God would present further revelation to add to His Word. The Bible begins with the very beginning of humanity—Genesis—and ends with the end of humanity as we know it—Revelation. Everything in between is for our benefit as believers, to be empowered with God's truth in our daily living. We know this from 2 Timothy 3:16–17, "All Scripture is God-breathed and is useful for teaching, rebuking, correcting and training in righteousness, so that the man of God may be thoroughly equipped for every good work."

If further books were added to the Bible, that would mean the Bible we have today is incomplete—that it does not tell us everything we need to know. Although it only applies directly to the book of Revelation, Revelation 22:18–20 teaches us an important truth about adding to God's Word: "I warn everyone who hears the words of the prophecy of this book: If anyone adds anything to them, God will add to him the plagues described in this book. And if anyone takes words away from this book of prophecy, God will take away from him his share in the tree of life and in the holy city, which are described in this book."

We have all that we need in the current 66 books of the Bible. There is not a single situation in life that cannot be addressed by Scripture. What was begun in Genesis finds conclusion in

Revelation. The Bible is absolutely complete and sufficient. Could God add to the Bible? Of course He could. However, there is no reason, biblically or theologically, to believe that He is going to do so, or that there is any need for Him to do so.

Chapter 4

QUESTIONS ABOUT
TRANSLATING THE BIBLE

Contents

Question: How does the translation process impact the inspiration, inerrancy, and infallibility of the Bible?

Answer: This question deals with three very important issues: inspiration, preservation, and translation.

The doctrine of the inspiration of the Bible teaches that Scripture is "God-breathed"; that is, the words are His. God personally superintended the writing process, guiding the human authors so His complete message was recorded for us. The Bible is truly God's Word. During the writing process, the personality and writing style of each author was allowed expression; however, God so directed the writers that the 66 books they produced were free of error and exactly what God wanted us to have. (See 2 Timothy 3:16 and 2 Peter 1:21.)

Of course, when we speak of "inspiration," we are referring only to the process by which the original documents were composed. After that, the doctrine of the preservation of the Bible takes over. If God went to such great lengths to give us His Word, surely He would also take steps to preserve that Word unchanged. What we see in history is that God did exactly that.

Jewish scribes painstakingly copied the Old Testament Hebrew Scriptures. Groups such as the Sopherim, the Zugoth, the Tannaim, and the Masoretes had a deep reverence for the texts they were copying. Their reverence was coupled with strict rules governing their work: the type of parchment used, the size of the columns, the kind of ink, and the spacing of words were all prescribed. Writing anything from memory was expressly forbidden, and the lines, words, and even the individual letters were methodically counted as a means of double-checking accuracy. The result of all this was that the words written by Isaiah's pen are still available today. The discovery of the Dead Sea Scrolls clearly confirms the precision of the Hebrew text.

The same is true for the New Testament Greek text. Thousands of Greek texts, some dating back to nearly AD 117, are available. The slight variations among the texts—not one of which affects an article of faith—are easily reconciled. Scholars have concluded that the New Testament we have at present is virtually unchanged from the original writings. Textual scholar Sir Frederic Kenyon said about the Bible, "It is practically certain that the true reading of every doubtful passage is preserved ... this can be said of no other ancient book in the world."[4]

This brings us to the translation of the Bible. Translation is an interpretative process, to some extent. When translating from one language to another, choices must be made. Should it be the more exact word, even if the meaning of that word is unclear to the modern reader? Or should it be a corresponding thought, at the expense of a more literal reading?

As an example, in Colossians 3:12, Paul says we are to put on "bowels of mercies" (KJV). The Greek word for "bowels," which is literally "intestines," comes from a root word meaning "spleen." The KJV translators chose a literal translation of the word. The translators of the NASB chose "heart of compassion"—the "heart" being what today's reader thinks of as the seat of emotions. The NIV simply puts "compassion."

So, the KJV is the most literal in the above example, but the other translations certainly do justice to the verse. The core meaning of the command is to have compassionate feelings.

Most translations of the Bible are done by committee. This helps to guarantee that no individual prejudice or theology will affect the decisions of word choice, etc. Of course, the committee itself may have a particular agenda or bias (such as those producing the current "gender-neutral" or "inclusive-language" mistranslations). But there is still plenty of good scholarship being done, and many good translations are available.

Having a good, honest translation of the Bible is important. A proper translating team will have done its homework and will let the Bible speak for itself.

As a general rule, the more literal translations, such as the KJV, NKJV, ASB, and NASB, have less "interpretative" work. The "freer" translations, such as the NIV, NLT, and CEV, by necessity do more "interpretation" of the text, but are generally more readable. Then there are the paraphrases, such as The Message and The Living

Bible, which are not really translations at all but one person's retelling of the Bible.

So, with all that in view, are translations of the Bible inspired and inerrant? The answer is, no, they are not. God nowhere extends the promise of inspiration to translations of His Word. While many of the translations available today are superb in quality, they are not inspired by God, and are not perfect. Does this mean we cannot trust a translation? Again, the answer is no. Through careful study of Scripture, with the Holy Spirit's guidance, we can properly understand, interpret, and apply Scripture. Again, due to the faithful efforts of dedicated Christian translators (and of course the oversight of the Holy Spirit), most translations available today are excellent and trustworthy. The fact that we cannot ascribe inerrancy to a translation should motivate us toward even closer study and away from blind devotion to any particular translation.

Question: What is the Critical Text?

Answer: The Critical Text is a Greek New Testament that draws from a group of ancient Greek manuscripts and their variants in an attempt to preserve the most accurate wording possible. In addition to the Critical Text, there are two other Greek texts used for producing English Bibles: the Majority Text and the *Textus Receptus*.

Until the late 1800s, Erasmus's *Textus Receptus* (Latin for "received text") was the foremost Greek text from which the New Testament was derived. (The King James Version and New King James Version are based on the *Textus Receptus*.) In 1881, two prominent scholars, Brooke Foss Westcott and Fenton J. A. Hort, printed their *New Testament in Greek*, later known as the Critical Text. Dismissing the *Textus Receptus* as an inferior text rife with errors, Westcott and Hort compiled a new Greek text, with a special focus on two fourth-century manuscripts, the *Codex Vaticanus* and the *Codex Sinaiticus*.

Westcott and Hort's Critical Text became the standard Greek text used for modern translation for nearly two generations. The Critical Text was the chief manuscript used to produce the

English Revised Version and the later American Standard Version. Today, the updated and revised Critical Text is the basis for the New International Version, the New American Standard Bible, the English Standard Version, and virtually every other modern English translation of the Bible.

The Critical Text has been accepted, on the whole, as being the most accurate in duplicating the original text of the New Testament. Great care was taken in compiling the Critical Text. Here is a sampling of the rules Westcott and Hort followed:

1. The reading[a] is less likely to be original if it shows a disposition to smooth away difficulties.
2. Readings are approved or rejected by reason of the quality, and not the number, of supporting witnesses.
3. The preferred reading best explains the existence of other readings.
4. The preferred reading makes the best sense; that is, it best conforms to the grammar and is most congruous with the purport of the rest of the sentence and of the larger context.

With the discovery of new manuscript evidence, the Critical Text has been revised many times. Currently, an updated version, called the Nestle-Aland text (now in its 28th edition), is the Critical Text in common use, along with the *Greek New Testament* published by the United Bible Societies (UBS).

In summary, the Critical Text reflects an effort to discover the wording of the original Greek manuscripts of the New Testament by comparing/contrasting all of the existing manuscripts and using logic and reason to determine the most likely original readings. While no human effort will ever produce an absolutely perfect copy of the original manuscripts of the New Testament,

---

[a] A "reading" is a particular variant among several choices; e.g., one manuscript might read, "King David," while another manuscript reads, "David the king." The compiler must choose the more accurate reading— and by "more accurate," it is meant "nearer the original."

the Critical Text is very likely extremely close to what the New Testament authors wrote.

Question: What is the Masoretic Text?

Answer: The Hebrew text of the Old Testament is called the Masoretic Text because, in its present form, it is based upon the Masora—the textual tradition of the Jewish scholars known as the Masoretes (or Masorites). The Masoretes were rabbis who made it their special work to correct the faults that had crept into the text of the Old Testament during the Babylonian captivity and to prevent its being corrupted by any future alterations.

There is a great difference of opinion as to when the Masoretic Text was written, but it was probably accomplished between the seventh and 11th centuries AD. Several editions existed, varying considerably, but the one considered authoritative in Judaism is that of Jacob ben-chayim ibn Adonijah, who carefully sifted and arranged the previous works on the subject. His work was published in 1524.

Although existing copies of the Masoretic Text date back only to the tenth century AD, two other important textual evidences bolster confidence in its accuracy. The first is the succession of discoveries of the Qumran manuscripts (the Dead Sea Scrolls), beginning in 1947. Some of these manuscripts were several centuries older than any previously known. The second evidence is the comparison of the Masoretic text to the Greek translation called the Septuagint, written around 200–150 BC. The oldest existing manuscripts of the Septuagint date back to the fourth century AD. Both the Septuagint and the Dead Sea Scrolls reveal an amazing consistency with the Masoretic Text, assuring us that God was indeed sovereignly protecting His Word through thousands of years of copying and translating.

Question: What is the Majority Text?

Answer: The Majority Text, also known as the Byzantine and Ecclesiastical Text, is a compilation of Greek New Testament manuscripts based on the reading found in a majority of the manuscripts. As the New Testament was copied hundreds of times over 1,500 years, the scribes, as careful as they were, occasionally made mistakes. The vast majority of these mistakes are misspellings or changes in a preposition. It is important to remember, though, that no doctrine of the Christian faith is put into doubt by these textual issues. The testimony of the thousands of manuscripts over 1,500 years is entirely consistent on all the key points of the Christian faith.

Of course, it is vital that our Bibles are as accurate as possible. The accuracy of the manuscripts used plays a large role in determining the accuracy of the translation. While a misspelling or an inserted character is not usually critical to the meaning of a verse, there are times when it can be. This is where the science of textual criticism comes in. The goal of textual criticism is to examine all of the available manuscripts and, by comparison and contrast, to determine what the original text truly said.

The Majority Text method within textual criticism could be called the "democratic" method. Essentially, each Greek manuscript has one vote. All the manuscripts vote on all the variant readings, and whichever variant has the most votes wins. At first glance, the Majority Text method would *seem* to be the best way to identify the original reading. The problem is that the Majority Text method does not take into account two important factors: 1) the age of the manuscripts and 2) the location of the manuscripts.

1. **The age of the manuscripts.** The more times a manuscript is copied, the more likely it is that errors will occur. A first-generation copy—one that was copied directly from the original—is likely to be closer to the original than a tenth-generation copy. Manuscripts from the second, third, and fourth centuries should be far closer to the originals than manuscripts from the 12th, 13th, and 14th centuries. The problem is that the majority of the manuscripts currently available are from the 12th, 13th, and 14th centuries. To illustrate, let's say there is a man named James Smith, and you are attempting to discover James Smith's middle name.

Who would be a better source of information, James Smith's great-great-great-great-great-grandchildren or James Smith's son? Of course, James Smith's son would likely have better knowledge. Similarly, a second- or third-generation copy of the New Testament is far more likely to be correct than a twelfth- or thirteenth-generation copy.

2. **The location of the manuscripts.** The vast majority of Christians through the centuries have lived in Western and Eastern Europe. For cultural, theological, and political reasons, the Western and Eastern churches split. The Western church became the Roman Catholic Church while the Eastern church became the Orthodox Church. A few centuries after Christ, the Western church began using Latin as its primary language. The Eastern church continued using Greek as its primary language for another thousand years (and, in some places, even to today). Textual critics have found that manuscripts discovered in one part of the world tend to be very similar to other manuscripts from that same part of the world, likely due to their originating from the same source. Since the Eastern church continued using Greek for 1,000+ years longer than the Western church, there are significantly more Greek manuscripts found in Eastern Europe than in Western Europe. And these Eastern Greek manuscripts (the Byzantine manuscripts) are all very similar to each other. In compiling the Majority Text, the Eastern Greek manuscripts had far greater weight than the Western Greek manuscripts, due to their sheer numbers. However, if the thousands of Latin manuscripts from the Western church were thrown into the Majority Text equation, the results of the "voting" would be far more balanced and would actually tilt away from the Eastern/Byzantine reading.

To further illustrate, let's say there are two copies of a document, Document A and Document B, with minor differences between them due to copyist mistakes. Document A is copied 100 times, while Document B is copied three times. If we use the Majority Text method, the Document A copies would have 100 votes, while the Document B copies would only have 3 votes. The Document A copies would win every time. However, since Document A and Document B are both first-generation copies themselves, Document A and Document B and their "descendants" should be given equal weight in determining the original reading.

The factors of age and location, then, result in "majority rule" not being the best method in textual criticism. A better method would take into account all factors: majority, age, location, difficulty of the reading, and which variant best explains the origin of the other variants. This method exists and is known as the "Eclectic Text" or "Critical Text." Other than the King James Version and New King James Version (which are based on the *Textus Receptus*), all modern English translations are based on the Eclectic Text.

To summarize, the Majority Text is based on a method within textual criticism that uses "majority rule" to determine which variant is most likely to be original. While the Majority Text method does result in the most likely original reading in most instances, it should not be employed universally or exclusively. There are many other important factors in determining which variant is closest to the original.

Question: What is the Septuagint?

Answer: The Septuagint (abbreviated as LXX) is a translation of the Hebrew Bible into the Greek language. The name "Septuagint" comes from the Latin word for "seventy." The tradition is that 70 (or 72) Jewish scholars were the translators behind the Septuagint. The Septuagint was translated in the third and second centuries BC in Alexandria, Egypt. As Israel was under the authority of the Greek Empire for several centuries, the Greek language became more widely spoken in Palestine. By the second and first centuries BC, most people in Israel spoke Greek as their primary language. That is why the effort was made to translate the Hebrew Bible into Greek—so those who did not know Hebrew could have the Scriptures in a language they could understand. By the time of Christ, the Septuagint had "replaced" the Hebrew Bible as the Scriptures most people used. The Septuagint represents the first major effort at translating a significant religious text from one language into another.

It is interesting to note that, many times, when the New Testament quotes from the Old Testament, the wording is that of the Septuagint. For example, in Acts 7:42–43, when Stephen quotes Amos 5:26–27, he uses the LXX translation.

As faithful as the Septuagint translators strived to be in accurately rendering the Hebrew text into Greek, some translational differences arose. In comparing an Old Testament verse with its New Testament citation, we sometimes notice a discrepancy. For example, in Matthew 21:16, Jesus quotes from the LXX version of Psalm 8:2: "From the lips of children and infants you have ordained praise." However, our English text of Psalm 8:2 reads, "From the lips of children and infants you have ordained praise because of your enemies." The difference is slight and is due to decisions made by the translators of the Septuagint.

The fact that Jesus and the apostles used the Septuagint and the New Testament authors felt comfortable, under the direction of the Holy Spirit, in quoting the Septuagint should assure us that a translation of the original languages of the Bible is still the authoritative Word of God.

Question: What is the *Textus Receptus?*

Answer: The *Textus Receptus* (Latin for "Received Text") is a Greek New Testament that provided the textual base for the vernacular translations of the Reformation Period. It was a printed text, not a hand-copied manuscript, created in the 15th century to fill the need for a textually accurate Greek New Testament.

As the Christian message was carried abroad, the books of the New Testament were taken along and translated into the languages of the people to whom the message was given. In the transmission of the text, copies were made, mostly by Christians who were not trained in the task; therefore, not too much attention was given to the correctness of the copies. As the number of copies in the different languages proliferated, the various versions were found to contain many differences and discrepancies. Eventually, it became obvious that there was a need for a standardized Greek text from which all translations could be made.

Needless to say, the invention of the printing press with movable type in the mid-15th century revolutionized the world of literature. The first book to be printed, in 1456, was the Latin Vulgate, also known as the Gutenberg Bible. Bible scholars at that time were little concerned about the Greek text of the New Testament; the Latin Vulgate was their Bible.

Then, in the late 15th century, the ancient Greek language—forgotten for hundreds of years in the West—was rediscovered in the geographical area of the Latin Church. As Western scholars rediscovered Greek, the Latin Vulgate was subjected to a critical examination in comparison with the Greek original. Scholars discovered numerous mistranslations or outright errors in the Vulgate. This provided another reason for printing the New Testament in its original language, Koine Greek.

Erasmus, a 15th-century Dutch theologian, working at great speed in order to beat to press another Greek New Testament being prepared in Spain, gathered together what hand-copied Greek manuscripts he could locate. He found five or six, the majority of which were from the 12th century. In his haste, Erasmus did not even transcribe the manuscripts; he merely made notes on the manuscripts themselves and sent them to the printers. The entire Greek New Testament was printed in about six to eight months and published in 1516. Erasmus' work became a best-seller, despite its errors, and the first printing was soon sold out. A second edition was published in 1519 with some of the errors corrected.

Erasmus published two other editions in 1527 and 1535. Stung by criticism that his work contained numerous textual errors, he incorporated readings from the Greek New Testament published in Spain in later editions of his work. Erasmus' Greek text became the standard in the field, and other editors and printers continued the work after his death in 1536. In 1633, another edition was published. In the publisher's preface, in Latin, we find the following words: *Textum ergo habes, nun cab omnibus receptum*, which is translated as "the [reader] now has the text that is received by all." From that publisher's notation have come the words "Received Text." The *Textus Receptus* became the dominant Greek text of the New Testament for the following 250 years. It was not until the publication of the Westcott and Hort Greek New Testament in 1881 that the *Textus Receptus* lost its position.

The reason the *Textus Receptus* lost its prominent position as a basis of biblical textual interpretation was the inception of textual criticism. Influential scholars paved the way for the acceptance of a critical text. The work of Westcott and Hort brought about the final dethronement of the *Textus Receptus* and the establishment of a critical text. The *Textus Receptus* is not a "bad" or misleading text, either theologically or practically. But it was limited by the small number of manuscripts that had been available to Erasmus. Even with the shortcomings of the *Textus Receptus*, it was three centuries before scholars won the struggle to replace this hastily assembled text with one better reflecting the New Testament autographs.

Many consider the King James Version of the Bible to be the crown of English Bibles. And it is true that the KJV is unparalleled as a work of English literature—its beautiful phrasing and majestic cadences influenced the English-speaking world for centuries. The Greek text used in preparing the KJV was the *Textus Receptus*. Earlier, the *Textus Receptus* influenced the Reformation, as both Luther and Tyndale used it to translate the Scriptures. Luther used the second edition of the Erasmus New Testament for his German translation, and Tyndale utilized the third edition for his English translation.

Regardless of one's position on the *Textus Receptus*, it is evident that it had great influence on preserving God's inspired Word through many centuries. Textual criticism of the Scriptures is so important that all students of the Word of God should utilize its principles. We must fulfill the biblical mandate, "Do your best to present yourself to God as one approved, a workman who does not need to be ashamed and who correctly handles the word of truth" (2 Timothy 2:15).

Question: Should Mark 16:9–20 be in the Bible?

Answer: Although the vast majority of later Greek manuscripts contain Mark 16:9–20, the gospel of Mark ends at verse 8 in two of the oldest and most respected manuscripts, the Codex Sinaiticus and Codex Vaticanus. Scholars who consider the older manuscripts to be more accurate have concluded that scribes added these verses later. The King James Version of the Bible and the New King James Version contain verses 9–20 because the KJV used the *Textus Receptus* as the basis for its translation. Since the 1611 publication of the KJV, however, the older manuscripts have been discovered.

The internal evidence from this particular passage also casts doubt on Mark as the author. For one thing, the transition between verses 8 and 9 is abrupt and awkward. The Greek word translated "now" that begins verse 9 should link it to what follows, as the use of the word *now* does in the other Synoptic Gospels. However, what follows doesn't continue the story of the women referred to in verse 8, and describes instead Jesus' appearing to Mary Magdalene. There is no transition there, but rather an abrupt change atypical of the continuity of Mark's narrative. Further, for Mark to introduce Mary Magdalene here as though for the very first time (verse 9) is odd because she had already been introduced earlier (Mark 15:40, 47; 16:1).

Furthermore, the vocabulary is not consistent with Mark's gospel. These last verses do not read the same as the rest of the book. There are eighteen words here that are never used anywhere else in the book, and the structure is very different from the familiar structure of Mark's writing. The title "Lord Jesus," used in verse 19, is never used anywhere else by Mark. Also, the signs mentioned in verses 17–18 do not appear elsewhere in any of the four Gospels. In no post-resurrection account of Jesus is there any discussion of picking up serpents, speaking with tongues, casting out demons, drinking poison, or laying hands on the sick. So, both internally and externally, there is evidence that these verses are foreign to Mark.

Both external and internal evidence point to point to Mark not being the author of this passage. In reality, ending his gospel in verse 8 with the description of the amazement of the women at the tomb is entirely consistent with the rest of Mark's narrative. Amazement at the Lord Jesus is a theme in the gospel of Mark (for examples, see Mark 1:22, 27; 2:12; 4:41; 5:15, 33, 42; 6:51). Some early scribe, however, apparently felt the need to add a more conventional ending.

Question: Why are the newer translations of the Bible missing verses?

Answer: If you compare the King James and New King James Versions with the newer translations (e.g., the New International Version, New American Standard, New Living Translation, etc.), you will notice that several verses are missing from the newer translations or set apart in some way. Examples are John 5:4, Acts 8:37, 1 John 5:7, and Mark 16:9–20. Usually, these passages are bracketed within the text or found in the footnotes. Why do these translations not have these verses? Are the newer translations taking verses out of the Bible?

The answer is that the translators did not believe these verses should have been in the Bible to begin with. Since the KJV was translated in AD 1611, many biblical manuscripts have been discovered that are older than those the KJV was based on. When Bible scholars researched these manuscripts, they discovered some differences. It seems that, over the course of 1,500 years, some words, phrases, and even sentences were added to the Bible, either intentionally or accidentally. The verses mentioned above are simply not found in the oldest manuscripts. Based on the idea that the older manuscripts are closer to the original and therefore more reliable, the newer translations removed these verses or placed them in footnotes or in the margin.

It is important to remember, however, that the verses in question are of minor significance. None of them change in any way the crucial themes of the Bible, nor do they have any impact on the Bible's core doctrines—Jesus' death, burial, and resurrection; Christ as the only the way of salvation; heaven and hell; sin and redemption; and the nature and character of God.

Chapter 5

QUESTIONS ABOUT THE INSPIRATION AND INERRANCY OF THE BIBLE

Contents

What does it mean that the Bible is infallible? What is biblical infallibility?

Do I have to believe the Bible is inerrant to be saved?

Has the Bible been corrupted, altered, edited, revised, or tampered with?

Does the inerrancy of the Bible only apply to the original manuscripts?

Is the doctrine of preservation biblical?

What is the doctrine of the sufficiency of Scripture? What does it mean that the Bible is sufficient?

What is *sola scriptura*?

Question: Why should I believe the Bible?

Answer: The Bible makes claims about the creation of the universe, the nature of the God who created the universe and reigns supremely over it, and the fate of mankind. If these claims are true, then the Bible is the most important book in the history of mankind. If the Bible is true, then it holds the answers to life's biggest questions: "From where did I come?" "Why am I here?" and "What happens to me when I die?" The importance of the Bible's message demands it receive fair consideration, and the truthfulness of its message is observable, testable, and able to withstand scrutiny.

The writers of the Bible claim that the Bible is God's very Word. The apostle Paul writes that "all Scripture is God-breathed" (2 Timothy 3:16). That is to say, all the words recorded in the original writing of Scripture originated from the mouth of God before ever reaching the minds and pens of the biblical writers. The apostle Peter also writes that "prophecy never had its origin in the will of man, but men spoke from God as they were carried along by the Holy Spirit" (2 Peter 1:21). The phrase "carried along" is indicative of a sail being propelled by the wind. That is, the Holy Spirit directed the writing of Scripture. The Bible does not originate with man and is, then, a product of God and carries the authority of God.

At this point, it is important not to let circular reasoning become the justification for believing the Bible. We cannot say that one should believe the Bible simply because the Bible says it should be believed. If, however, these claims are found true whenever it is possible to test their veracity during historical and scientific discovery, then the internal claims of the Bible's own trustworthiness are more compelling. The internal evidence works in tandem with the external.

The internal evidence of Scripture's veracity provides many compelling arguments for why one should believe the Bible. First, the unique message of the Bible sets it apart from other religious texts. The Bible, for instance, teaches that mankind is inherently evil and deserving of eternal death. If man were responsible for the content of the Bible, the view of humanity would not be so dark—we tend to make ourselves look good. The Bible also teaches that humans can do nothing of themselves to remedy their natural state. This, too, goes against human pride.

The unity of the biblical message is further reason for why one should believe the Bible. The Bible was written over a period of approximately 1,500 years, with at least 40 human writers, most of whom did not know each other and were from varying backgrounds (king, fisherman, tax collector, shepherd, etc.). The Bible was written in various environments (desert, prison, royal court, etc.). Three different languages were used to write the Bible, and, despite covering controversial subjects, it carries one harmonious message. The circumstances surrounding the writing of the Bible would seem to guarantee its fallibility, and, yet, the message from Genesis to Revelation is strikingly consistent.

Another reason why one should believe the Bible is its accuracy. The Bible should not be confused with a science textbook, but that does not mean that the Bible does not speak to issues that are scientific in nature. The water cycle was described in Scripture centuries before it was a scientific discovery (Isaiah 55:10). In some cases science and the Bible have seemed to be at odds with each other. Yet, when science has advanced, the scientific theories have proved wrong and the Bible proved right. For example, it used to be standard medical practice to bleed patients as a cure for illness. Many people died because of excessive blood loss. Now medical professionals know that bloodletting as a cure for most diseases is counterproductive. The Bible always taught that "the life of a creature is in the blood" (Leviticus 17:11).

The Bible's claims concerning world history have also been substantiated. Skeptics used to criticize the Bible for its mention of the Hittite people (e.g., 2 Kings 7:6). The lack of any archeological evidence to support the existence of a Hittite culture was often cited as a rebuttal against Scripture. In 1876, however, archaeologists discovered evidence of the Hittite nation, and by the early 20th century the vastness of the Hittite nation and its influence in the ancient world were common knowledge.

The scientific and historical accuracy of the Bible is important evidence of the Bible's trustworthiness, but the Bible also contains fulfilled prophecies. Some of the biblical writers made assertions about future events centuries in advance. If any one of the events predicted had occurred, it would be astounding. But the Bible contains many, many prophecies. Some of the predictions were fulfilled in a short amount of time (Abraham and Sarah had a son, Peter denied Jesus three times, Paul was a witness for Jesus in Rome, etc.). Other predictions were fulfilled hundreds of years later. One person could not have reasonably fulfilled the around 300 messianic prophecies Jesus fulfilled unless some greater power was involved. Specific prophecies like Jesus' birthplace, activities, manner of death, and resurrection demonstrate the preternatural accuracy of Scripture.

When it is put to the test, the Bible is proved true in every area. Its truth extends to the spiritual, as well. That means when the Bible says the Hittite nation existed, we can believe there were Hittites; and when the Bible teaches that "all have sinned" (Romans 3:23) and the "wages of sin is death" (Romans 6:23), we need to believe that, too. And when the Bible tells us that "God demonstrates his own love for us in this: While we were still sinners, Christ died for us" (Romans 5:8) and that "whoever believes in [Jesus] shall not perish but have eternal life" (John 3:16), we can and should believe that, as well.

Question: Is the Bible truly God's Word?

Answer: The answer to this question will not only determine how we view the Bible and its importance in our lives, but it will also eternally impact our destiny. If the Bible is truly God's Word, then we should cherish it, study it, obey it, and fully trust it. If the Bible is the Word of God, then to dismiss it is to dismiss God Himself.

The fact that God gave us the Bible is an evidence and illustration of His love for us. The Bible is God's revelation to us. The term *revelation* implies that God communicated to mankind what He is like and how we can have a right relationship with Him. These are things we could not have known had God not divinely revealed them to us in the Bible. The Bible contains everything man needs to know about God in order to have a right relationship with Him. If the Bible is truly the Word of God, then it is the final authority for all matters of faith, religious practice, and morality.

How can we know the Bible is the Word of God and not just a good book? What is unique about the Bible that sets it apart from all other religious books? Is there any evidence that the Bible is truly God's Word? These types of questions must be seriously examined if we are to determine the validity of the Bible's claim to be the very Word of God, divinely inspired, and totally sufficient for all matters of faith and practice. There can be no doubt that the Bible does claim to be the very Word of God. This is clearly seen in Paul's commendation to Timothy: "… from infancy you have known the holy Scriptures, which are able to make you wise for salvation through faith in Christ Jesus. All Scripture is God-breathed and is useful for teaching, rebuking, correcting and training in righteousness, so that the man of God may be thoroughly equipped for every good work" (2 Timothy 3:15–17).

There are both internal and external evidences that the Bible is truly God's Word. The internal evidences are those things within the Bible that testify of its divine origin. One internal evidence that the Bible is truly God's Word is its unity. Even though it is really 66 individual books, written on three continents, in three different languages, by more than 40 authors who came from many walks of life, and over a period of approximately 1,500 years, the Bible remains one unified book from beginning to end without contradiction. This unity is unique and sets it apart from all other books. It is evidence of the divine origin of the words that God moved men to record.

Another internal evidence that indicates the Bible is truly God's Word is the many prophecies contained within its pages. The Bible contains hundreds of detailed prophecies relating to the future of individual nations, certain cities, and mankind. Other prophecies concern the coming the Messiah, the Savior of all who would believe in Him. Unlike the prophecies found in other religious books or those by men such as Nostradamus, biblical prophecies are extremely detailed. There are over three hundred prophecies concerning Jesus Christ in the Old Testament. Not only was it foretold where He would be born and His lineage, but also how He would die and that He would rise again. There simply is no logical way to explain the fulfilled prophecies in the Bible other than to attribute them to divine origin. There is no other religious book that even comes close to the amount of predictive prophecy the Bible contains.

A third internal evidence of the divine origin of the Bible is its unique authority and power. While this evidence is more subjective than the first two, it is no less a powerful testimony of the divine origin of the Bible. The Bible's authority is unlike that of any other book ever written. This power is seen in the way countless lives have been transformed by God's Word. Drug addicts have been cured by it, derelicts and deadbeats transformed by it, hardened criminals reformed by it, sinners rebuked by it, and hate turned to love by it. The Bible does possess a dynamic and transforming power that is only possible because it is truly God's Word.

There are also external evidences that indicate the Bible is truly the Word of God. One is the historicity of the Bible. Because the Bible details historical events, its truthfulness and accuracy are subject to verification like any other historical document. Through archaeological evidences and other ancient texts, the historical accounts of the Bible have been proven time and time again to be accurate. In fact, all the archaeological and manuscript evidence supporting the Bible makes it the best-documented book from the ancient world. The fact that the Bible accurately records historically verifiable events is a great indication of its truthfulness when dealing with religious subjects and doctrines and helps substantiate its claim to be the very Word of God.

Another external evidence that the Bible is truly God's Word is the integrity of its human authors. In studying the lives of the men who recorded God's words, we find them to be honest and sincere. The fact that they were willing to die excruciating deaths for what they believed demonstrates that these ordinary men truly believed God had spoken to them. The men who wrote the New Testament, and many hundreds of other believers, had seen and spent time with Jesus Christ after He had risen from the dead (1 Corinthians 15:6). Seeing the risen Christ had a tremendous impact on them. They went from hiding in fear to being willing to die for the message God had revealed to them. Their lives and deaths testify to the fact that the Bible truly is God's Word.

Another external evidence that the Bible is truly God's Word is its indestructibility. Because of its importance and its claim to be the very Word of God, the Bible has suffered more vicious attacks and attempts to destroy it than any other book in history. From early Roman Emperors like Diocletian, through communist dictators and on to modern-day atheists and agnostics, the Bible has outlasted all of its attackers and is still today the most widely published book in the world.

Throughout time, skeptics have regarded the Bible as mythological, but archaeology has confirmed it as historical. Opponents have attacked its teaching as primitive and outdated, but its moral and legal concepts have had a positive influence on societies and cultures throughout the world. It continues to be attacked by pseudo-science, psychology, and political movements, yet it remains just as true and relevant today as it was when it was first written. It is a book that has transformed countless lives and cultures throughout the last 2,000 years. No matter how its opponents try to attack, destroy, or discredit it, the Bible remains; its veracity and impact on lives is unmistakable. It should not surprise us that, no matter how the Bible is attacked, it always comes out unscathed. After all, Jesus said, "Heaven and earth will pass away, but my words will never pass away" (Mark 13:31). After looking at the evidence, one can say without a doubt that, yes, the Bible is truly God's Word.

Question: What does it mean that the Bible is inspired?

Answer: When people speak of the Bible as inspired, they are referring to the fact that God divinely influenced the human authors of the Scriptures in such a way that what they wrote was the very Word of God. In the context of the Scriptures, the word *inspiration* simply means "God-breathed" (2 Timothy 3:16). The result of inspiration is that the Bible truly is the Word of God and the Bible is unique among all other books.

While there are different views as to the extent to which the Bible is inspired, there can be no doubt that the Bible itself claims that every word in every part of the Bible comes from God (1 Corinthians 2:12–13; 2 Timothy 3:16–17). This view of the Scriptures is often referred to as "verbal plenary" inspiration. That means the inspiration extends to the very words themselves (verbal)—not just to concepts or ideas—and that the inspiration extends to all parts of Scripture and all subject matters of Scripture (plenary). Some people believe only parts of the Bible are inspired or only the concepts that deal with religion are inspired, but these views of inspiration fall short of the Bible's claims about itself. Full verbal plenary inspiration is an essential characteristic of the Word of God.

The extent of inspiration can be clearly seen in 2 Timothy 3:16, "All Scripture is God-breathed and is useful for teaching, rebuking, correcting and training in righteousness, so that the man of God may be thoroughly equipped for every good work." This verse tells us that God inspired all Scripture and that it is profitable to us. It is not just the parts of the Bible that deal with religious doctrines that are inspired, but every word from Genesis to Revelation. Because it is inspired by God, Scripture is authoritative in establishing doctrine and sufficient for teaching man how to be in a right relationship with God. The Bible claims not only to be inspired by God, but also to have the supernatural ability to change us and make us "complete." What more could we need?

Another verse that deals with the inspiration of Scripture is 2 Peter 1:21: "For prophecy never had its origin in the will of man, but men spoke from God as they were carried along by the Holy Spirit." This verse helps us to understand that, even though God used men with their distinctive personalities and writing styles, God divinely inspired the very words they wrote. Jesus Himself confirmed the verbal plenary inspiration of the Scriptures when He said, "Do not think that I have come to abolish the Law or the Prophets; I have not come to abolish them but to fulfill them. I tell you the truth, until heaven and earth disappear, not the smallest letter, not the least stroke of a pen, will by any means disappear from the Law ..." (Matthew 5:17–18). In these verses, Jesus is reinforcing the accuracy of Scripture down to the smallest detail and the slightest punctuation mark, because it is the very Word of God.

Since the Scriptures are the inspired Word of God, we can conclude that they are also inerrant and authoritative. A correct view of God will lead us to a correct view of His Word. Because God is all-powerful, all-knowing, and completely perfect, His Word will by its very nature have the same characteristics. The same verses that establish the inspiration of the Scriptures also establish that without a doubt the Bible is what it claims to be—the undeniable, authoritative Word of God to humanity.

Question: Is there proof for the inspiration of the Bible?

Answer: Here are some evidences that the Bible is inspired ("God-breathed"), as declared in 2 Timothy 3:16:

1. **Fulfilled prophecy.** God spoke to men telling them of things He would bring about in the future. Some of those things have already occurred. Others have not. For example, the Old Testament contains more than 300 prophecies concerning Jesus Christ's first coming. There is no doubt that these are prophecies from God, because the manuscripts are dated from before the birth of Christ. These were not written after the fact, but beforehand.

2. **The unity of Scripture.** The Bible was written by approximately 40 human authors over a period of about 1,600 years. These men were quite diverse. Moses was a political leader; Joshua, a military leader; David, a shepherd; Solomon, a king; Amos, a herdsman and fruit picker; Daniel, a prime minister; Matthew, a tax collector;

Luke, a medical doctor; Paul, a rabbi; Peter, a fisherman; and the list goes on. The Bible was also written under a variety of circumstances across 3 different continents: Europe, Asia, and Africa. Yet the great themes of Scripture are maintained in all the writings. The Bible does not contradict itself. There is no way, apart from the Holy Spirit supervising the writing of the Bible, that this could have been accomplished.

Contrast this with the Islamic Qur'an. It was compiled by one individual, Zaid bin Thabit, under the guidance of Mohammed's father-in-law, Abu-Bekr. Then, in AD 650, a group of Arab scholars produced a unified version and destroyed all variant copies to preserve the unity of the Qur'an. The Bible was unified from the time of its writing. The Qur'an had unity forced upon it by human editors.

3. **Realistic character portrayal.** The Bible presents its heroes truthfully with all of their faults and weaknesses. It does not glorify men as other religions do their heroes. Reading the Bible, one realizes that the people it describes have problems and do wrong just as we do. What made the heroes of the Bible great was that they trusted in God. For instance, David is described as "a man after his (God's) own heart" (1 Samuel 13:14). Yet David committed adultery (2 Samuel 11:1–4) and murder (2 Samuel 11:14–25). This information could have easily been omitted from Scripture, but the God of truth included it.

4. **Historical accuracy.** Archaeological findings support the history recorded in Scripture. Though many detractors throughout history have tried to find archaeological evidence to disprove the Bible, they have failed. It is easy to say that Scripture is untrue; proving it to be untrue is another matter and, in fact, has not been done. Sir William Mitchell Ramsay, a former atheist and skeptic, has documented in great detail the historical reliability of the New Testament, especially the book of Acts. Also of interest are the writings of Titus Flavius Josephus, a Jewish

historian who wrote during the first century AD. Josephus records some events that coincide with Scripture, thus bolstering the validity of the biblical narrative.

The Bible's claims of being from God should not be understood as circular reasoning (see Exodus 14:1; Leviticus 4:1; Numbers 4:1; Deuteronomy 4:2; Isaiah 1:10; Jeremiah 11:1–3; Ezekiel 1:3; 1 Corinthians 14:37; 1 Thessalonians 2:13; 2 Peter 1:16–21). The testimony of reliable witnesses—particularly Jesus, but also Moses, Joshua, David, Daniel, and Nehemiah in the Old Testament, and John and Paul in the New Testament—affirms the authority and verbal inspiration of the Holy Scriptures. Considering the evidence, we wholeheartedly accept the Bible as being from God (2 Timothy 3:16).

Question: What are the different theories of biblical inspiration?

Answer: Inspiration is one of the most important doctrines in Christianity. We hold the Bible to be inspired by God, and, as such, it is our infallible guide for faith and practice. If that guide is not "God-breathed" but simply the work of the human imagination, then there is no compelling reason to follow its doctrines and moral guidelines.

The reason we hold the Bible to be our guide for faith and practice can be summed up in one biblical passage: "All Scripture is inspired by God and profitable for teaching, for reproof, for correction, for training in righteousness; so that the man of God may be adequate, equipped for every good work" (2 Timothy 3:16–17 NASB). We notice two things regarding Scripture from this verse: 1) it is "inspired by God," and 2) it is "profitable" for Christian living. We can come up with definitions for the various things Scripture is profitable for (reproof, correction, etc.). What really needs to be determined is what is meant by "inspired by God."

There are four views of inspiration: 1) the neo-orthodox view, 2) the dictation method view, 3) the limited inspiration view, and 4) the plenary verbal inspiration view.

The neo-orthodox view of inspiration is based on the neo-orthodox view of God's transcendence. Neo-orthodoxy teaches that God is so completely different from us (i.e., utterly transcendent) that the only way we could ever know Him is through His revelation to us. This view of the transcendence of God is so restrictive that it denies any concept of natural theology (i.e., that God can be known through His creation). Furthermore, it denies that the Bible is the Word of God. Rather, the Bible is a witness, or mediator, to the Word of God, which is God Himself. The words in the Bible aren't God's words, but God can use them to speak to individuals. Basically, the words in the Bible are fallible words written by fallible men.

From what we can see, the neo-orthodox view of inspiration is no view of inspiration at all. If the Bible is the fallible product of fallible men, then it really has no value—at least, not any more than other books written by men. God could just as well "speak" to us through works of fiction as He could through the Bible, according to the neo-orthodox view.

Another theory is the dictation method of inspiration. This view sees God as the author of Scripture and the individual human agents as scribes taking dictation. God spoke, and man wrote it down. This view has some merit, as we know there are portions of Scripture in which God essentially says, "Write this down" (e.g., Jeremiah 30:2). But not all Scripture was created that way. Luke states in the preamble to his gospel that he performed detailed research into the events of the life of Jesus before writing his work (Luke 1:1–4). Many of the prophetic books read like journals of the prophets' lives. The bottom line is that the dictation method only explains certain portions of Scripture, but not all of it or even most of it.

In a way, the limited inspiration view is the opposite of the dictation view. Whereas the dictation theory sees Scripture as primarily the work of God with the human agent in the role of scribe, the limited inspiration theory sees Scripture as primarily the work of man with "limited" inspiration from God. God guides the human authors but allows them the freedom to express themselves in their works. This view asserts that, while there may be factual and historical errors in the Bible, the Holy Spirit guided the authors so that no doctrinal errors resulted. But here is the problem with limited inspiration: how can one trust the Bible in doctrinal concerns when it is prone to error in its historical accounts? The reliability of the entire Bible is called into doubt in this view. If we cannot trust a literary work to get mundane details right, how can we trust it in the weightier issues? This view also seems to ignore the fact that the Bible's story of redemption, from Genesis to Revelation, is told against the backdrop of human history—the doctrine is interwoven within the history. One cannot say that the historical account is inaccurate yet believe the history contains even a kernel of doctrinal truth.

The final view, and the view of orthodox Christianity, is the view of verbal plenary inspiration. The word *plenary* means "complete or full," and *verbal* means "the very words of Scripture." So verbal plenary inspiration means that every single word in the Bible is the very word of God. Second Timothy 3:16–17 contains a unique Greek word, *theopneustos*, which literally means that Scripture is "God-breathed."

In another biblical passage, we see that "prophecy never had its origin in the will of man, but men spoke from God as they were carried along by the Holy Spirit" (2 Peter 1:21). This passage gives us a clue as to how God inspired the human authors. We see that men spoke (or wrote) "as they were carried along by the Holy Spirit." The verb translated "carried along" is also used of a sail's being filled with wind, carrying a boat along the water. This word is fitting, since the Greek word for "spirit" is also used for "wind." When the human authors were putting pen to paper, the Holy Spirit "carried them along" so that what they wrote were the "breathed-out" words of God. This means that, while the actual writings retain the personality of the individual authors (and that is obvious if you read the works of Paul compared to those of James or John or Peter), they contain the actual words of God.

In closing, it should be noted that there are some things inspiration is *not*:

1. Inspiration is not robotic dictation. The personality of the human authors is present in each of the writings.

2. The fact that individual personalities are present in the writings does not mean that God's "control" over them was imperfect. The Holy Spirit superintended the process so that the words written were the exact words God wanted, despite the fallibility of the human authors.

3. Inspiration is limited to the original writings (autographs) and does not cover the process of transmission. We know there are minute transmission errors in the copies of manuscripts, but these errors are grammatical and not substantive.

4. The inspiration of Scripture extends to the verbal level, meaning that it is not just the ideas or thoughts that are inspired, but the very words. Moreover, we don't speak of inspiration of Scripture as we would the "inspiration" of a great work of literature or music.

5. Finally, inspiration is limited to the specific works of the authors that are included in the biblical canon. Paul wasn't inspired, but the book of Romans was. Furthermore, not all letters of Paul were inspired, but only the ones the Holy Spirit chose to preserve (e.g., 2 Corinthians 7:8 mentions a letter from Paul of which we have no existing copies).

In a nutshell, verbal plenary inspiration is the orthodox view of the church, which says that every word of the Bible is fully inspired by God.

Question: Are the writings of the apostle Paul inspired (see 1 Corinthians 7:12)?

Answer: The bulk of conservative evangelical Christianity believes in the verbal plenary inspiration of Scripture, meaning that every single word of the Bible is "God-breathed" (2 Timothy 3:16). If biblical critics can claim that 1 Corinthians 7:12 is not inspired, but is rather Paul's opinion, what other passages could they claim to be the opinion of a human author and not the command of the divine Author? This issue strikes at the very heart of biblical authority.

Paul wrote this letter to a group of Christians dwelling in Corinth, a very corrupt city. Part of that corruption was due to the presence of the temple of Aphrodite, home to over 1,000 temple prostitutes. Given the paganism of the culture, it should be no surprise that many of the church congregation came out of an immoral lifestyle. The church of Corinth was made up of former fornicators, idolaters, adulterers, homosexuals, thieves, and drunkards (1 Corinthians 6:9–11).

When Paul gets into chapter 7 of his letter, he is answering a question the church had regarding sexual relations between men and women. With the cultural climate in their city, the Corinthians thought it would be a good thing for everyone to remain celibate. Paul agrees that celibacy is a good thing and even states that he wishes more people could be celibate, as he was. Paul is not disparaging marriage. He is simply stating the obvious benefits that singleness affords the ministry. However, Paul mentions that singleness is a gift from God, and not all have the gift (verse 7). For those currently married, Paul tells them to remain so, and in verse 10 Paul says, "Not I, but the Lord." This means that Paul is relating to the Corinthians a direct command from Jesus. This command comes from Jesus' teaching in the Gospels, in particular Matthew 5:32.

Finally, in verse 12, Paul addresses "mixed marriages"—those between a Christian and a non-Christian. The Corinthians might be tempted to divorce their unbelieving spouses, thinking that by doing so they would be purifying themselves. Paul tells the believing spouse to remain with the unbeliever, with the comment that the command comes from him, not from Jesus. But Paul is not offering his own "opinion" here. He is saying that Jesus never addressed this issue directly during His earthly ministry. The Gospels do not contain any direct teaching of Jesus touching on the case of a believing spouse married to an unbeliever. Jesus only gave one legitimate reason for divorce (Matthew 5:32; 19:9), and being married to an unbeliever was not it.

So the best answer is that Paul provided new revelation in an area that Jesus did not specifically address. That is why Paul says, "I, not the Lord." In other words, I, not Jesus, am giving you this command, although it is based on the principles Jesus taught. As extensive as Jesus' ministry was, He did not articulate everything regarding the Christian life. That is why He commissioned the apostles to carry on His ministry after His ascension, and that is why we have a God-breathed Bible, "so that the man of God may be thoroughly equipped for every good work" (2 Timothy 3:16–17).

Paul was responsible for much new revelation, although ultimately those revelations came from the Holy Spirit. In many of his epistles, Paul reveals "mysteries." The word *mystery* is a technical term that signifies some previously unrevealed truth that is now revealed, such as the church being comprised of both Jews and Gentiles (Romans 11:25) or the rapture (1 Corinthians 15:51–52). In 1 Corinthians 7:12 Paul is simply giving additional revelation regarding marriage. His command is as inspired as Jesus' words in the Gospels.

Question: How do we know that the Bible is the Word of God, and not the Apocrypha, the Qur'an, the Book of Mormon, etc.?

Answer: The question of which (if any) religious text is the true Word of God is of utmost importance. To avoid circular reasoning, the first question we must ask is, "How would we know if God communicated in the first place?" Well, God would have to communicate in a manner that people could understand. But then what would prevent people from making up their own messages and claiming a divine origin for them? It seems reasonable to think that, to authenticate His communication, God would have to verify it in a manner that could not be duplicated by mere humans—in other words, by miracles. This narrows the field considerably.

Helping us toward a determination that the Bible is absolute, divine truth is its supernatural evidence, including prophecy. God used prophets to speak and write down His Word, and God specified the mark of a true prophet: 100 percent accuracy (Deuteronomy 18:21–23). One example of fulfilled prophecy is Jeremiah 23:3, where God predicted that Israel would be re-gathered from the surrounding nations and made to prosper again. This is exactly what happened after the Babylonian Captivity in 538 BC and again in AD 1948, after World War II. The Jews returned to their land. This may not seem so astonishing until you realize that no other nation in history has been scattered from its homeland and returned! Israel has done it *twice*.

The book of Daniel predicts with amazing accuracy the coming of the four great kingdoms—Babylon, Medo-Persia, Greece, and Rome—centuries before some of those kingdoms came into being (a time span of over 1,000 years!). Daniel wrote details concerning how the nations would rule and be broken. His prophecies include the reigns of Alexander the Great and Antiochus Epiphanies.

In Ezekiel 26 we see in astonishing detail how the city of Tyre was to be destroyed: it would be torn down, and its debris would be thrown into the sea. When Alexander the Great marched on that area, he encountered a group of people holed up in a tower on an island off the coast near Tyre. He could not cross the channel to fight those in the tower. Rather than wait them out, the proud conqueror had his army build a land bridge to the island. It worked. His army crossed the channel and overthrew the stronghold. But where did they get enough stone for the land bridge? The rocks they used were the leftover rubble from the city of Tyre. Its stones were cast into the sea, just as Ezekiel had predicted almost 300 years earlier.

There are so many prophecies concerning the earthly ministry of Christ (over 270) that it would take more than a few pages to list them all. The Gospels show how each prophecy was fulfilled. Jesus, who affirmed the Bible as the Word of God, proved His reliability and deity by His resurrection (an historical fact not easily ignored).

Now consider the Qur'an. Its author, Muhammad, performed no miracles to confirm his message (even when he was asked to by his followers; Sura 17:91–95; 29:47–51). Only in much later tradition (called the Hadith) do any alleged miracles show up, and these are all quite fanciful (like Muhammad cutting the moon in half) and have no reliable testimony to confirm them. Further, the Qur'an contains clear historical errors. Muslims believe the Bible is inspired, but with some errors from editing (Sura 2:136, as well as Suras 13, 16, 17, 20, 21, 23, 25). The question they cannot adequately answer is, "*When* was the Bible corrupted?"

The Qur'an also has an insurmountable problem in that it accuses Christians of believing things that they do not believe. For example, the Qur'an teaches that Christians believe the Trinity is the Father, the Mother (Mary), and the Son (Sura 5:73–75, 116). The Qur'an also claims that Christians believe that God had sex with Mary in order to produce a son (Suras 2:116; 6:100–101; 10:68; 16:57; 19:35; 23:91; 37:149–151; 43:16–19). If the Qur'an is really from God, then it should at least be able to accurately report what Christians believe.

Joseph Smith, the author of the Book of Mormon, tried to do some miracles such as prophecy, but he failed several times. He foretold Christ's second coming in *History of the Church* (HC) 2:382. Smith preached that the coming of the Lord would be in 56 years (about 1891). Of course, the second coming did not occur in 1891. Smith also prophesied that several cities would be destroyed (*Doctrine and Covenants* 84:114–115). According to Smith, New York, Albany, and Boston were to be demolished if they rejected his "gospel." Joseph Smith himself went to New York, Albany, and Boston and preached there. These cities did not accept his message, yet they have not been destroyed. Another famous false prophecy of Joseph Smith is his "End of All Nations" (*Doctrine and Covenants* 87), concerning the Civil War. The South was supposed to call on Great Britain for aid, and as a result war would be poured out upon all nations—slaves would revolt; the inhabitants of the earth would mourn; famine, plague, earthquakes, thunder, lightning, and a full end of all nations would result. The South finally did revolt in 1861, but the slaves did not rise up, war was not poured out upon all nations, there was no worldwide famine, plague, or earthquake, and there was no "end of all nations."

The collection of writings Protestants call the Apocrypha ("hidden writings"), Roman Catholics call the deuterocanonical ("second canon") books. These books were written between 300 BC and AD 100, the Intertestamental Period between the inspired writing of the Old and New Testaments. The Roman Catholic Church "infallibly" accepted the Apocrypha into the Bible in 1546 at the Council of Trent. Of course, the Apocrypha would be covered under the evidence for the Bible, if these writings were truly inspired—but the evidence seems to indicate that they are not. In the Bible we find prophets of God whose messages are ratified by miracles or fulfilled prophecy (Deuteronomy 34:11; Romans 15:19; 2 Corinthians 12:12; Hebrews 2:4). What we find in the Apocrypha is just the opposite—no apocryphal book was written by a prophet; in fact, one book specifically states that it is *not* inspired (1 Maccabees 9:27)! No apocryphal book was included in the Hebrew Scriptures. Later biblical writers cite no apocryphal book as authoritative. There is no fulfilled prophecy in any apocryphal book. Finally, Jesus, who quoted from every section of Old Testament Scripture, never once quoted from the Apocrypha. Neither did any of His disciples.

The Bible so far outshines every competing source for being God's revelation that, if it were not God's Word, it would be impossible to choose among the leftovers.

Question: Does the Bible contain errors, contradictions, or discrepancies?

Answer: If we read the Bible at face value, without a preconceived bias for finding errors, we will find it to be a coherent, consistent, and relatively easy-to-understand book. Yes, there are difficult passages. Yes, there are verses that *appear* to contradict each other. Each biblical writer wrote with a different style, from a different perspective, to a different audience, for a different purpose. We should expect some minor differences. However, a difference is not a contradiction.

An "error" is only an error if there is absolutely no conceivable way the passages can be reconciled. For example, some people point to Mark 15:32 and Luke 23:40–42 as a "contradiction." Mark says the thieves crucified with Jesus insulted Him; Luke says that one of the thieves believed in Jesus. The difference between the two accounts is easily reconciled by taking into account the fact that Jesus was on the cross for three hours, and the thieves witnessed Jesus' demeanor the whole time. At the beginning of their time on the cross, both thieves reviled Jesus, but by the end of their ordeal, one of the thieves had seen the truth. Mark and Luke are complementary. One gives us a general (true) statement of the thieves' attitude; the other gives us further (true) information of what happened *later.*

Even if an answer to a Bible difficulty is not available right now, that does not mean it will never be available. Many critics have found that supposed historical errors in the Bible disappear with the discovery of further archaeological evidence. For example, historians used to question the Bible's mention of the Hittites (Judges 1:26); all such questions were laid to rest with the discovery of the remains of the Hittite civilization in the 1940s.

There are viable and intellectually plausible answers to every supposed Bible contradiction and error. Most people who claim that there are errors in the Bible have never read the Bible for themselves. The saddest thing is that most people who attack the Bible are not truly interested in answers. They do not seek the truth. They may even be aware of valid answers to their arguments, but they continue to attack God's Word.

So, what are we to do when someone approaches us with an alleged Bible error? 1) Prayerfully study the Scriptures and see if there is a simple solution; 2) do some research using some of the Bible commentaries, apologetic books, and biblical research websites available; 3) ask our pastors/church leaders for their input; and 4) trust God that His Word is truth and that there is a solution that simply has not been realized yet (2 Timothy 2:15; 3:16–17).

Question: Why is it important to believe in biblical inerrancy?

Answer: We live in a time that tends to shrug its shoulders when confronted with error. Instead of asking, like Pilate, "What is truth?" postmodern man says, "Nothing is truth" or perhaps "There is truth, but we cannot know it." We've grown accustomed to being lied to, and many people seem comfortable with the false notion that the Bible, too, contains errors.

The doctrine of biblical inerrancy is an extremely important one because the truth does matter. This issue reflects on the character of God and is foundational to our understanding of everything the Bible teaches. Here are some reasons why we should absolutely believe in biblical inerrancy:

1. **The Bible itself claims to be perfect.** "And the words of the LORD are flawless, like silver refined in a furnace of clay, purified seven times" (Psalm 12:6). "The law of the LORD is perfect" (Psalm 19:7). "Every word of God is flawless" (Proverbs 30:5). These claims of purity and perfection are absolute statements. Note that it doesn't say God's Word is "mostly" pure or Scripture is "nearly" perfect. The Bible argues for complete perfection, leaving no room for "partial perfection" theories.

2. **The Bible stands or falls as a whole.** If a major newspaper were routinely discovered to contain errors, it would be quickly discredited. It would make no difference to say, "All the errors are confined to page three." For a paper to be reliable in any of its parts, it must be factual throughout. In the same way, if the Bible is inaccurate when it speaks

of geology, why should its theology be trusted? It is either a trustworthy document, or it is not.

3. **The Bible is a reflection of its Author.** All books are. God Himself wrote the Bible as He worked through human authors in a process called "inspiration." "All Scripture is God-breathed" (2 Timothy 3:16; see also 2 Peter 1:21 and Jeremiah 1:2.)

   We believe that the God who created the universe is capable of writing a book. And the God who is perfect is capable of writing a perfect book. The issue is not simply "Does the Bible have a mistake?" but "Can God make a mistake?" If the Bible contains factual errors, then God is not omniscient and is capable of making errors Himself. If the Bible contains misinformation, then God is not truthful but is instead a liar. If the Bible contains contradictions, then God is the author of confusion. In other words, if biblical inerrancy is not true, then God is not God.

4. **The Bible judges us, not vice versa.** "For the word of God ... judges the thoughts and attitudes of the heart" (Hebrews 4:12). Notice the relationship between "the heart" and "the Word." The Word examines; the heart is being examined. To discount parts of the Word for any reason is to reverse this process. We become the examiners, and the Word must submit to our "superior insight." Yet God says, "But who are you, O man, to talk back to God?" (Romans 9:20).

5. **The Bible's message must be taken as a whole.** It is not a mixture of doctrine from which we are free to select. Many people like the verses that say God loves them, but they dislike the verses that say God will judge sinners. But we simply cannot pick and choose what we like about the Bible and throw the rest away. If the Bible is wrong about hell, for example, then who is to say it is right about heaven— or about anything else? If the Bible cannot get the details right about creation, then maybe the details about salvation cannot be trusted either. If the story of Jonah is a myth, then perhaps so is the story of Jesus. On the contrary, God

has said what He has said, and the Bible presents us a full picture of who God is. "Your word, O Lord, is eternal; it stands firm in the heavens" (Psalm 119:89).

6. **The Bible is our only rule for faith and practice.** If it is not reliable, then on what do we base our beliefs? Jesus asks for our trust, and that includes trust in what He says in His Word. John 6:67–69 is a beautiful passage. Jesus had just witnessed the departure of many who had claimed to follow Him. Then He turns to the twelve apostles and asks, "You do not want to leave too, do you?" At this, Peter speaks for the rest when he says, "Lord, to whom shall we go? You have the words of eternal life." May we have the same trust in the Lord and in His words of life.

None of what we have presented here should be taken as a rejection of true scholarship. We are commanded to study the Word (2 Timothy 2:15), and those who search it out are commended (Acts 17:11). Also, we recognize that there are difficult passages in the Bible, as well as sincere disagreements over interpretation. Our goal is to approach Scripture reverently and prayerfully, and when we find something we do not understand, we pray harder, study more, and—if the answer still eludes us—humbly acknowledge our own limitations in the face of the perfect Word of God.

Question: What does it mean that the Bible is infallible? What is biblical infallibility?

Answer: The word *infallible* means "incapable of error." If something is infallible, it is never wrong and thus absolutely trustworthy. Similarly, the word *inerrant*, also applied to Scripture, means "free from error." Simply put, the Bible never fails.

The Bible's origin lays claim to infallibility in the book of 2 Peter: "Above all, you must understand that no prophecy of Scripture came about by the prophet's own interpretation. For prophecy never had its origin in the will of man, but men spoke from God as they were carried along by the Holy Spirit" (2 Peter 1:20–21).

Also, we see infallibility implied in 2 Timothy 3:16–17: "All Scripture is God-breathed" and has the effect of producing servants of God who are "thoroughly equipped for every good work." The fact that God "breathed" Scripture insures that the Bible is infallible, for God cannot breathe out error. The fact that the Bible equips God's servants "thoroughly" for service shows that it guides us into truth, not error.

If God is infallible, then so will be His Word. The doctrine of Scripture's infallibility is based on an understanding of God's perfection of character. God's Word is "perfect, reviving the soul" (Psalm 19:7) because God Himself is perfect. Theologically, God is closely associated with His Word; the Lord Jesus is called "the Word" (John 1:14).

It should be noted that the doctrine of infallibility concerns only the original documents. Mistranslations, printing errors, and typos are obvious human mistakes and are easily spotted most of the time. However, what the biblical writers originally wrote was completely free from error or omission, as the Spirit superintended their task. God is truthful and perfectly reliable (John 14:6; 17:3), and so is His Word (John 17:17).

The Bible claims complete (as opposed to partial) perfection in Psalm 12:6, Psalm 19:7, Proverbs 30:5, and many other places. It is factual throughout and, in fact, judges us (rather than vice-versa): "The word of God is alive and active. Sharper than any double-edged sword, it penetrates even to dividing soul and spirit, joints and marrow; it judges the thoughts and attitudes of the heart" (Hebrews 4:12).

The Bible is the sole objective source of all God has given us about Himself and His plan for humanity. As God's infallible Word, the Bible is inerrant, authoritative, reliable, and sufficient to meet our needs.

Question: Do I have to believe the Bible is inerrant to be saved?

Answer: We are not saved by believing in the inspiration or inerrancy of the Bible. We are saved by believing in the Lord Jesus Christ as our Savior from sin (John 3:16; Ephesians 2:8–9; Romans 10:9–10). At the same time, though, it is only through the Bible that we learn about Jesus Christ and His death and resurrection on our behalf (2 Corinthians 5:21; Romans 5:8). We do not have to believe everything in the Bible in order to be saved—but we do have to believe in Jesus Christ, who is proclaimed by the Bible. We should definitely hold to the Bible as the Word of God, and we should absolutely believe everything the Bible teaches.

When people are first saved, they generally know very little about the Bible. Salvation is a process that begins with an understanding of our sinful state, not an understanding of the inerrancy of the Bible. Our consciences tell us that we are not able to stand before a holy God on our own merits. We know that we are not righteous enough for that, so we turn to Him and accept the sacrifice of His Son on the cross as payment for our sin. We place our full trust in Him. From that point on, we have a completely new nature, pure and undefiled by sin. God's Holy Spirit lives within our hearts, sealing us for eternity. We go forward from there, loving and obeying God more and more each day. Part of this "going forward" is feeding daily on His Word to grow and strengthen our walk with Him (1 Peter 2:2). The Bible alone has the power to perform this miracle in our lives.

If we believe and trust in the Person and work of the Lord Jesus Christ, as taught in the Bible, we are saved. When we trust in Jesus Christ, though, the Holy Spirit will work on our hearts and minds and will convince us that the Bible is true and is to be believed (2 Timothy 3:16–17). If there are doubts in our minds about the inerrancy of Scripture, the best way to handle them is to ask God to give us assurance about and confidence in His Word. He is more than willing to answer those who seek Him honestly and with their whole hearts (Matthew 7:7–8).

Question: Has the Bible been corrupted, altered, edited, revised, or tampered with?

Answer: The books of the Old Testament were written from approximately 1400 BC to 400 BC. The books of the New Testament were written from approximately AD 40 to AD 90. So, anywhere between 3,400 to 1,900 years have passed since a particular book of the Bible was written. In this time, the original manuscripts have been lost. They very likely no longer exist. Also during this time, the books of the Bible have been copied again and again. Copies of copies of copies have been made. In view of this, can we still trust the Bible?

When God originally inspired men to write His Word, it was God-breathed and inerrant (2 Timothy 3:16–17; John 17:17). The Bible nowhere applies this to copies of the original manuscripts. As meticulous as scribes were with the replication of the Scriptures, no one is perfect. As a result, minor differences arose in the various copies of the Scriptures. Of all of the thousands of Greek and Hebrew manuscripts that are in existence, no two were identical until the printing press was invented in the 1500s.

However, any unbiased document scholar will agree that the Bible has been remarkably well-preserved over the centuries. Copies of the Bible dating to the 14th century AD are nearly identical in content to copies from the third century AD. When the Dead Sea Scrolls were discovered, scholars were shocked to see how similar they were to other ancient copies of the Old Testament, even though the Dead Sea Scrolls were hundreds of years older than anything previously discovered. Even many hardened skeptics and critics of the Bible admit that the Bible has been transmitted over the centuries far more accurately than any other ancient document.

There is absolutely no evidence that the Bible has been revised, edited, or tampered with in any systematic manner. The sheer volume of biblical manuscripts makes it simple to recognize any attempts to distort God's Word. There is no major doctrine of the Bible that is put in doubt as a result of the minor differences that exist between manuscripts.

Can we trust the Bible? Absolutely! God has preserved His Word despite the unintentional failings and intentional attacks of human beings. We can have utmost confidence that the Bible we have today is the same Bible that was originally written. The Bible is God's Word, and we can trust it (Matthew 5:18).

Question: Does the inerrancy of the Bible only apply to the original manuscripts?

Answer: This is truly a difficult issue to grasp. Only the original autographs (original manuscripts written by the apostles, prophets, etc.) are under the divine promise of inspiration and inerrancy. The books of the Bible, as they were originally written under the inspiration of the Holy Spirit (2 Timothy 3:16–17; 2 Peter 1:20–21), were 100 percent inerrant, accurate, authoritative, and true. There is no biblical promise that copies of the original manuscripts would be equally inerrant or free from copyist errors. As the Bible has been copied thousands of times over thousands of years, some copyist errors have likely occurred.

How do we deal with this? First, it is important to remember that the biblical manuscripts we have today are in 99 percent agreement with one another. Yes, there are some minor differences, but the vast majority of the biblical text is identical from one manuscript to another. Most of the differences are in punctuation, word endings, minor grammatical issues, word order, etc.— issues easily explainable as scribal mistakes. But no important theological or biblical issue is thrown into doubt by any supposed error or contradiction. Biblical manuscripts from the 15th century agree completely with manuscripts from the third century. We can have absolute confidence that the Bible we have today is almost exactly identical to what the apostles and prophets wrote over 2,000 years ago.

Second, we should not be quick to say, "Oh, that is just a scribal error." The vast majority, if not all, of Bible "errors" can be explained in a logical and believable manner. Those that cannot be explained, or are very difficult to explain, could very well have an answer that we simply do not know at this point. Just because we cannot find a solution does not mean that a solution does not exist. Believing there to be a scribal error must be the absolute last resort in any supposed Bible "error."

Ultimately, though, it is possible that errors have crept into our modern manuscripts and translations of the Bible. Copyists and translators are human beings, and they make mistakes. The evidence of the Bible's incredibly accurate transmission is a testimony to its inspiration and preservation by God.

Can we trust the Bible? Absolutely! The Bible translations we have today are God's Word. The Bible today is just as authoritative as it was in the first century AD. We can completely trust the Bible as being God's message to us today. Yes, the biblical promises of inspiration and inerrancy only apply directly to the original manuscripts. But that does not negate the accuracy and authority of our modern Bibles. Through the centuries, the Bible has been preserved with great care. God's Word endures forever, despite small typos and the occasional mistake of a copyist or translator.

Question: Is the doctrine of preservation biblical?

Answer: The doctrine of Scriptural preservation teaches that the Lord has kept His Word intact from the time of its writing until today. We can trust the Scriptures because God has sovereignly overseen the process of transmitting the text through the centuries. The *Westminster Confession of Faith* promotes this doctrine, saying that the Bible was "inspired by God and by his singular care and providence kept pure in all ages" (ch. 1, § 8).

The doctrine of biblical preservation can be seen as a natural outgrowth of the doctrine of biblical inspiration. For why would God inspire men to write exactly what He wanted and then fail to preserve those words for posterity? To deny the fact of biblical preservation is to accept that there may be "lost" books of the Bible that somehow were not preserved.

We should mention that we do not possess the original manuscripts, or autographs, today. What we do have are thousands of copied manuscripts. These copies contain some differences, but most of those differences are extremely small and insignificant, and none of them in any way affect the basic teachings or meaning of God's Word. The dissimilarities are mostly things like spelling variations and word order. Of course, a variant spelling does not affect the accuracy of Scripture, nor does it mean that God has not preserved His Word.

The ancient scribes, whose job was to make exact copies of Scripture, were very meticulous. One example of their scrupulous precision is their practice of counting all the letters in a given book and noting the middle letter of the book. After completing their copy of a book, the scribes would count all the letters in the fresh copy, finding the middle letter to make sure it matched the original. They employed other such time-consuming and painstaking methods to ensure accuracy.

Further, Scripture attests to God's plan to preserve His Word. In Matthew 5:18, Jesus said, "I tell you the truth, until heaven and earth disappear, not the smallest letter, not the least stroke of a pen, will by any means disappear from the Law until everything is accomplished." Jesus couldn't make that promise unless He was sure God would preserve His Word. Jesus also said, "Heaven and earth will pass away, but my words will never pass away" (Matthew 24:35; Mark 13:31; Luke 21:33). Whatever happens, God's Word will stand, and it will accomplish what God has planned.

The prophet Isaiah, through the power of the Holy Spirit, stated that God's Word will abide forever. "The grass withers and the flowers fall, but the word of our God stands forever" (Isaiah 40:8). This is reaffirmed in the New Testament as Peter quotes Isaiah and refers to Scripture as "the word that was preached to you" (1 Peter 1:24–25). Neither Isaiah nor Peter could make such statements without understanding God's preservation of Scripture.

When the Bible speaks of God's Word remaining forever, it cannot mean that it is hidden away in some vault in heaven. God's Word was given specifically for mankind, and it would not be fulfilling its purpose if it were not available to us. "For everything that was written in the past was written to teach us, so that through endurance and the encouragement of the Scriptures we might have hope" (Romans 15:4). A person cannot be saved apart from the gospel, which is recorded in God's Word (1 Corinthians 15:3–4). Therefore, in order for the gospel to be proclaimed "to the ends of the earth" (Acts 13:47), the Word must be protected. Through the supernatural preservation of His Word, God saw to it that the message the apostles preached is the same message we proclaim today.

Question: What is the doctrine of the sufficiency of Scripture? What does it mean that the Bible is sufficient?

Answer: The doctrine of the sufficiency of Scripture is a fundamental tenet of the Christian faith. To say the Scriptures are sufficient means that the Bible is all we need to equip us for a life of faith and service (2 Peter 1:3). The Bible presents God's intention to restore the broken relationship between Himself and humanity through His Son Jesus Christ. The Bible teaches us of faith, election, and salvation by Jesus' death on the cross and His subsequent resurrection. No other writings are necessary for this good news to be understood, nor are any other writings required to equip us for a life of faith. Man lives "on every word that comes from the mouth of God" (Matthew 4:4).

By "Scripture," Christians mean both Old and New Testaments. The apostle Paul declared that the Scriptures "are able to make you wise for salvation through faith in Christ Jesus. All Scripture is God-breathed and is useful for teaching, rebuking, correcting and training in righteousness, so that the man of God may be thoroughly equipped for every good work" (2 Timothy 3:15–17). If Scripture is "God-breathed," then it is not man-breathed. Although it was penned by men, those "men spoke from God as they were carried along by the Holy Spirit" (2 Peter 1:21). No man-made writing is sufficient to equip us for every good work; only the Word of God can do that. Furthermore, if the Scriptures are sufficient to *thoroughly* equip us, then nothing more is needed.

Colossians 2 discusses the dangers a church faces when the sufficiency of Scripture is denied or when extra-biblical writings are given equal status with Scripture. Paul warned the church at Colosse, "See to it that no one takes you captive through hollow and deceptive philosophy, which depends on human tradition and the basic principles of this world rather than on Christ" (Colossians 2:8). Jude is even more direct: "Although I was very eager to write to you about the salvation we share, I felt I had to write and urge you to contend for the faith that was once for all entrusted to the saints" (Jude 1:3). Notice the phrase "once for all." This makes it clear that no other writings, no matter how godly the pastor, theologian, or denominational church they may come from, are to be seen as equal to or completing the Word of God. The Bible contains all that is necessary for the believer to understand the character of God, the nature of man, and the doctrines of sin, heaven, hell, and salvation through Jesus Christ.

Perhaps the strongest verses on the sufficiency of the Bible come from the book of Psalms. In Psalm 19:7–14, David rejoices in God's Word, declaring it to be perfect, trustworthy, right, radiant, enlightening, sure, and altogether righteous. Since the Bible is "perfect," it has no equal and needs no improvement.

The sufficiency of Scripture is under attack today, and, sadly, that attack comes far too often from our own churches. Some churches neglect the Word of God in their pursuit of new models of church growth, new revelations, and new psychological theories. All the while, Jesus says, "My sheep listen to my voice; I know them, and they follow me" (John 10:27). The church doesn't need to follow fads; we only need to follow Jesus' voice.

Question: What is *sola scriptura*?

The phrase *sola scriptura* is from the Latin; *sola* having the idea of "alone" or "only," and the word *scriptura* meaning "writings"— referring to the Scriptures. *Sola scriptura* means that Scripture alone is authoritative for the faith and practice of the Christian. The Bible is complete, authoritative, and true. "All Scripture is

God-breathed and is useful for teaching, rebuking, correcting and training in righteousness" (2 Timothy 3:16).

Sola scriptura was the rallying cry of the Protestant Reformation. For centuries the Roman Catholic Church had made its traditions superior to the Bible. This resulted in many practices that were in fact contradictory to the Bible. Some examples are prayer to saints and Mary, the immaculate conception, transubstantiation, infant baptism, indulgences, and papal authority. Martin Luther, the founder of the Lutheran Church and father of the Protestant Reformation, publicly rebuked the Catholic Church for its unbiblical teachings. The Catholic Church threatened Martin Luther with excommunication (and death) if he did not recant. Luther's reply was, "Unless therefore I am convinced by the testimony of Scripture, or by the clearest reasoning, unless I am persuaded by means of the passages I have quoted, and unless they thus render my conscience bound by the Word of God, I cannot and will not retract, for it is unsafe for a Christian to speak against his conscience. Here I stand, I can do no other; may God help me! Amen!"

The primary Catholic argument against *sola scriptura* is that the Bible does not explicitly teach *sola scriptura*. Catholics argue that the Bible nowhere states that it is the only authoritative guide for faith and practice. While this is true, they fail to recognize a crucially important issue. We know that the Bible is the Word of God. The Bible declares itself to be God-breathed, inerrant, and authoritative. We also know that God does not change His mind or contradict Himself. So, while the Bible itself may not explicitly argue for *sola scriptura*, it most definitely does not allow for traditions that contradict its message. *Sola scriptura* is not as much of an argument against tradition as it is an argument against unbiblical or anti-biblical doctrines. The only way to know for sure what God expects of us is to stay true to what we know He has revealed—the Bible. We can know, beyond the shadow of any doubt, that Scripture is true, authoritative, and reliable. The same cannot be said of tradition.

The Word of God is the only authority for the Christian faith. Traditions are profitable only when they are based on Scripture and are in full agreement with Scripture. Traditions that contradict the Bible are not of God and are not a valid aspect of the Christian faith. *Sola scriptura* is the only way to avoid subjectivity and keep personal opinion from taking priority over the teachings of the Bible. The essence of *sola scriptura* is basing one's spiritual life on the Bible alone and rejecting any tradition or teaching that is not in full agreement with the Bible. Second Timothy 2:15 declares, "Do your best to present yourself to God as one approved, a workman who does not need to be ashamed and who correctly handles the word of truth."

Sola scriptura does not nullify the concept of church traditions. Rather, *sola scriptura* gives us a solid foundation on which to base church traditions. There are many practices, in both Catholic and Protestant churches, that are the result of traditions and not the explicit teaching of Scripture. It is good, and even necessary, for the church to have traditions. Traditions play an important role in clarifying and organizing Christian practice. At the same time, in order for these traditions to be valid, they must be in agreement with God's Word. They must be based on the solid foundation of the teaching of Scripture. The problem with the Roman Catholic Church, and many other churches, is that they base traditions on traditions that are based on traditions that are based on traditions, often with the initial tradition not being in full harmony with the Scriptures. That is why Christians must always go back to *sola scriptura*, the authoritative Word of God, as the only solid basis for faith and practice.

On a practical matter, a frequent objection to the concept of *sola scriptura* is the fact that the canon of the Bible was not officially agreed upon for at least 250 years after the church was founded. Further, the Scriptures were not available to the masses for over 1,500 years after the church was founded. How, then, were early Christians to use *sola scriptura*, when they did not even have the full Scriptures? And how were Christians who lived before the invention of the printing press supposed to base their faith and practice on Scripture alone if there was no way for them to have a complete copy of the Scriptures? This issue is further compounded by the high rates of illiteracy throughout history.

The problem with these objections is that they essentially say that Scripture's authority is based on its availability. This is not the case. Scripture's authority is universal; because it is God's Word, it is His authority. The fact that Scripture was not readily available, or that people could not read it, does not change the fact that Scripture is God's Word. Further, rather than this being an argument against *sola scriptura*, it is actually an argument for what the church should have done, instead of what it did. The early church should have made producing copies of the Scriptures a high priority. While it was unrealistic for every Christian to possess a complete copy of the Bible, it was possible that every church could have some, most, or all of the Scriptures available to it. Early church leaders should have made studying the Scriptures their highest priority so they could accurately teach it. Even if the Scriptures could not be made available to the masses, at least church leaders could be well-trained in the Word of God. Instead of building traditions upon traditions and passing them on from generation to generation, the church should have copied the Scriptures and taught the Scriptures (2 Timothy 4:2).

Again, traditions are not the problem. Unbiblical traditions are the problem. The availability of the Scriptures throughout the centuries is not the determining factor. The Scriptures themselves are the determining factor. We now have the Scriptures readily available to us. Through the careful study of God's Word, it is clear that many church traditions that have developed over the centuries are in fact contradictory to the Word of God. This is where *sola scriptura* applies. Traditions that are based on and in agreement with God's Word can be maintained. Traditions that are not based on or disagree with God's Word must be rejected. *Sola scriptura* points us back to what God has revealed to us in His Word. *Sola scriptura* ultimately points us back to the God who always speaks the truth, never contradicts Himself, and always proves Himself to be dependable.

Chapter 6

QUESTIONS ABOUT BIBLE TRANSLATIONS

Contents

Question: Why are there so many Bible translations, and which is the best?

Answer: The fact that there are so many English Bible translations is both a blessing and a problem. It is a blessing in that the Word of God is available to any English speaker who needs it in an easy-to-understand, accurate translation. It is a problem in that the different translations can create controversy and issues in Bible studies, teaching situations, etc. The differences between the translations can also be a cause of division within the church body.

It is probably wise to have access to at least two or three of the major translations for comparison's sake: KJV (King James Version), NIV (New International Version), NASB (New American Standard Bible), NKJV (New King James Version), ESV (English Standard Version), NLT (New Living Translation). If a verse or passage in one translation is a little confusing, it can be helpful to compare it side-by-side with another version. It is difficult to say which translation is the "best." "Best" would be determined by a combination of the translation method you personally prefer and your interpretation of the textual data underlying your translation. For example, the KJV and NASB have attempted to take the underlying Hebrew and Greek words and translate them into the closest corresponding English words (word-for-word), while the NIV and NLT have attempted to take the original thought presented in Greek and Hebrew and express that thought in English (thought-for-thought). Many of the other translations attempt to "meet in the middle" between those two methods. Paraphrases such as *The Message* or *The Living Bible* can be used to gain a different perspective on the meaning of a verse, but they should not be used as a primary Bible translation.

There are many more Bible translations than the six mentioned above. It is wise to have a personal method for determining whether a particular Bible translation is accurate. A good technique is to have a set of Scripture verses you know well, and look those verses up in a translation you are investigating. A good idea is to look at some of the most common verses that speak of the deity of Christ (John 1:1, 14; 8:58; 10:30; Titus 2:13) to make sure a Bible translation is true to the Word of God. Despite the multitudes of English Bible translations, we can be confident that the original Word of God is truth, and that it will accomplish His purposes (Isaiah 55:11; 2 Timothy 3:16–17; Hebrews 4:12).

Question: Should I use a paraphrase of the Bible?

Answer: A paraphrase is a retelling of something in your own words. A paraphrase of the Bible is different from a translation in that a translation attempts (to varying degrees) to communicate as word-for-word or as thought-for-thought as possible. A paraphrase takes the meaning of a verse or passage of Scripture and attempts to express the meaning in "plain language"—essentially, the words the author of the paraphrase would use to say the same thing. A popular example of a Bible paraphrase is *The Message* by Eugene Peterson.

Many people use paraphrases as their "reading Bible," preferring to read straight through as they would a novel. This can be particularly helpful in long narrative passages such as those found in Genesis, 1 and 2 Kings, and 1 and 2 Chronicles. Then they use actual translations, such as the New American Standard Bible, New King James Version, and New International Version, for in-depth reading and study.

Should you use a paraphrase? A paraphrase of the Bible should not be used as a Christian's primary Bible. We have to remember that a paraphrase is what the author thinks the Bible says, not necessarily what the Bible says. Eugene Peterson did a fair job on *The Message*, but there are many passages in *The Message* that do not accurately render the original meaning of the text. A paraphrase of the Bible should essentially be used as a commentary on the Bible, as a way to get another perspective. A paraphrase, though, should not be viewed as the Bible, but as an author's *idea* of what the Bible says.

Question: What are the different English Bible versions?

Answer: Depending on how one distinguishes a different Bible version from a revision of an existing Bible version, there are as many as 50 different English versions of the Bible. The question then arises: Is there really a *need* for so many different English versions of the Bible? The answer is, of course, that there is no *need* for 50 different English versions of the Bible. At the same time, there is nothing wrong with there being multiple versions of the Bible in a language. In fact, multiple versions of the Bible can actually be an aid in understanding the message of the Bible.

There are two primary reasons for the different English Bible versions. First, the English language changes and develops over time, making updates to an English version necessary. If a modern reader were to pick up a 1611 King James Version of the Bible, he would find it to be virtually unreadable. Everything from the spelling to syntax, grammar, and phraseology is very different. Linguists state that the English language has changed more in the past 400 years than the Greek language has changed in the past 2,000 years. Several times in church history, believers have gotten "used" to a particular Bible version and become fiercely loyal to it, resisting any attempts to update or revise it. This occurred with the Septuagint, the Latin Vulgate, and more recently, the King James Version. Fierce loyalty to a particular version of the Bible is counterproductive. When the Bible was written, it was written in the common language of the people at that time. When the Bible is translated, it should be translated into how a people/language group speaks and reads at that time, not how it spoke hundreds of years ago.

Second, there are different translation methodologies for how to best render the original Hebrew, Aramaic, and Greek into English. Some Bible versions translate as literally (word-for-word) as possible, which is commonly known as formal equivalence. Some Bible versions translate less literally, in more of a thought-for-thought method, commonly known as dynamic equivalence. All of the different English Bible versions are at different points of the formal equivalence vs. dynamic equivalence spectrum. The New American Standard Bible and the King James Version would be to the far end of the formal equivalence side, while paraphrases such as *The Living Bible* and *The Message* would be to the far end of the dynamic equivalence side.

The advantage of formal equivalence is that it minimizes the translator's inserting his own interpretations into the passages. The disadvantage of formal equivalence is that it often produces a translation so woodenly literal that it is not easily read or understood. The advantage of dynamic equivalence is that it usually produces a more readable and understandable Bible version; however, dynamic equivalence sometimes results in "this is what I think it means" instead of "this is what it says." Neither method is right or wrong. The best Bible version is likely produced through a balance of the two methodologies.

Listed below are the most common English versions of the Bible. In choosing which Bible version(s) you are going to use, do research, discuss the matter with Christians you respect, read the Bibles for yourself, and ultimately, ask God for wisdom regarding which Bible version He desires you to use.

King James Version (KJV)
New International Version (NIV)
New American Standard Bible (NASB)
New King James Version (NKJV)
English Standard Version (ESV)
New Living Translation (NLT)
Holman Christian Standard Bible (HCSB)
New Revised Standard Version (NRSV)
New Century Version (NCV)
New English Bible (NEB)
New English Translation (NET)
American Standard Version (ASV)
Revised Standard Version (RSV)
Good News Bible (GNB)/Today's English Version (TEV)
Easy-To-Read Version (ERV)
Complete Jewish Bible (CJB)
Bible in Basic English (BBE)
Amplified Bible (AMP)

Contemporary English Version (CEV)
God's Word Translation (GW)
New International Reader's Version (NIrV)
Today's New International Version (TNIV)
21st Century King James Version (KJ21)
Revised English Bible (REB)
Jerusalem Bible (JB)
New American Bible (NAB)
The Living Bible (TLB)
The Message (MSG)

Question: What is the Latin Vulgate Bible?

Answer: "The Vulgate" is the popular name given to the standard Latin version of the Bible, a translation usually attributed to Jerome, a fourth-century Roman Catholic priest. Before Jerome's time, as the number of Latin-speaking Christians grew, the Bible was translated into Latin so the Christians of the time could understand it. It is believed that the first Latin translation was completed around AD 200, although no manuscripts from this era exist today. The first Latin manuscripts were surely created in North Africa, for it seems that the church in North Africa was Latin-speaking from the start, while the churches in Asia and Europe were predominantly Greek-speaking.

Two centuries later, Pope Damasus I commissioned Jerome to produce one standard Latin text of the Bible; there were as many different Latin versions of the Bible as there were different forms of the text, and Damasus wanted the church to have a standard version to promote universal doctrine. Jerome completed the translation in AD 400, and his version was known as the *editio vulgate* (the current text of Holy Scripture), because he used the common (or vulgar) language of early medieval times.

Jerome started by revising the Gospels, using the Greek manuscripts available. He did this because of the vast differences he found in the various Latin texts. About the same time, he started revising the Old Testament by using the Septuagint (a

Greek version of the Old Testament). Jerome also translated the Old Testament into Latin by using the Hebrew text, a task he did without permission of the church. The present Vulgate contains elements belonging to every period of its development. The texts used to create the modern Vulgate include the following:

1. An unrevised Old Latin text of the Book of Wisdom, Ecclesiasticus, 1 and 2 Maccabees, and Baruch.
2. An Old Latin form of the Psalter, which Jerome corrected using the Septuagint.
3. Jerome's free translation of the books of Job and Judith.
4. Jerome's translation from the Hebrew Old Testament, excluding the Psalter.
5. An Old Latin revision of the Gospels from Greek manuscripts.
6. An Old Latin New Testament, revised.

Some of the books mentioned belong to a group known as the "Apocrypha," books of Jewish origin that are normally considered to lie outside the canon of the Old Testament.

Question: What is the KJV-Only Movement? Is the King James Version the only Bible we should use?

Answer: Many people have strong and serious objections to the translation methods and textual basis for newer translations and therefore take a strong stance in favor of the King James Version. Others are equally convinced that the newer translations are an improvement over the KJV in their textual basis and translation methodology. Got Questions Ministries does not want to limit its ministry to those of the "KJV-Only" persuasion. Nor do we want to limit ourselves to those who prefer the NIV, NASB, NKJV, etc. The purpose of this article is not to argue against the use of the King James Version. Rather, the focus of this article is to contend with the idea that the King James Version is the only Bible English speakers should use.

The KJV-Only Movement claims loyalty to the *Textus Receptus*, a Greek New Testament manuscript compilation completed in the 1500s. To varying degrees, KJV-Only advocates argue that God guided Erasmus (the compiler of the *Textus Receptus*) to come up with a Greek text that is perfectly identical to what was originally written by the biblical authors. However, upon further examination, it can be seen that KJV-Only advocates are not loyal to the *Textus Receptus*, but rather only to the KJV itself. The New Testament of the New King James Version is based on the *Textus Receptus*, just as the KJV is. Yet, KJV-Only advocates label the NKJV just as heretical as they do the NIV, NASB, etc.

Beyond the NKJV, other attempts have been made to make minimal updates to the KJV, "modernizing" the archaic language while using the same Greek and Hebrew manuscripts. These attempts are rejected nearly as strongly as the NKJV and the other newer Bible translations. KJV-Only advocates have no desire or plan to update the KJV in any way. The KJV certainly contains English that is outdated, archaic, and sometimes confusing to modern English speakers and readers. It would be fairly simple to publish an updated KJV with the archaic words and phrases updated into modern, 21st-century English. However, any attempt to edit the KJV in any way results in accusations from KJV-Only advocates of heresy and perversion of the Word of God.

When the Bible is translated for the first time into a new language today, it is translated into the language that culture speaks and writes presently, not the way they spoke and wrote 400 years ago. The same should be true in English. The KJV Bible was written in the common, ordinary language of the people at that time (the 1600s). Bible translations today should follow the same principle. That is why Bible translations must be updated and revised as languages develop and change.

Our loyalties should be to the original manuscripts of the Old and New Testaments, written in Hebrew, Aramaic, and Greek. Only the original autographs are inspired. A translation is only an attempt to take what is said in one language and communicate it in another. The modern translations do well in taking the meaning of the original languages and communicating it in a way we can understand in English. However, none of the modern translations are perfect. Every one contains verses that are at least somewhat mistranslated. By comparing and contrasting several different translations, it is easier to grasp what a verse is saying. Our loyalty should not be to any one English translation but to the inspired, inerrant Word of God (2 Timothy 3:16–17).

Chapter 7

QUESTIONS ABOUT STUDYING THE BIBLE

Contents

115

How should the different genres of the Bible impact how we interpret the Bible?

Does the Bible contain allegory?

What is biblical typology?

Is there any validity to Bible codes?

What is the biblical doctrine of illumination?

Question: Why should we read/study the Bible?

Answer: We should read and study the Bible because it is God's Word to us. The Bible is literally "God-breathed" (2 Timothy 3:16). In other words, it is God's very words. There are so many questions that philosophers have asked that God answers for us in Scripture. What is the purpose to life? Where did I come from? Is there life after death? How do I get to heaven? Why is the world full of evil? Why do I struggle to do good? In addition to these "big" questions, the Bible gives much practical advice: What do I look for in a mate? How can I have a successful marriage? How can I be a good friend? How can I be a good parent? What is success and how do I achieve it? How can I change? How can I live so that I do not look back with regret? How can I handle the unfair circumstances and bad events of life victoriously?

We should read and study the Bible because it is completely reliable and without error. The Bible is unique among so-called "holy" books in that it does not merely give moral teaching and say, "Trust me." Rather, we have the ability to test it by checking the hundreds of detailed prophecies that it makes, by verifying the historical accounts it records, and by testing the scientific facts it relates. Those who say the Bible has errors have their ears closed to the truth.

Jesus once asked which is easier to say: "Your sins are forgiven you" or "Rise, take up your bed and walk" (see Matthew 9:1–8). He then proved He had the ability to forgive sins (something undemonstrable) by healing the paralytic (something demonstrable). Similarly, we are given assurance that God's Word is true when it discusses untestable, spiritual topics by showing itself true in those areas we *can* test, such as history, science, and prophecy.

We should read and study the Bible because God does not change and because mankind's nature does not change; the Bible is as relevant for us today as it was when it was written. We find, as we read the pages of biblical history, that whether we are talking about individuals or whole societies, "there is nothing new under the sun" (Ecclesiastes 1:9). And while mankind continues to seek love and satisfaction in all the wrong places, God—our good and gracious Creator—tells us what will bring us lasting joy. His revealed Word, the Bible, is so important that Jesus said of it, "Man does not live on bread alone, but on every word that comes from the mouth of God" (Matthew 4:4). In other words, if we want to live life to the fullest, as God intended, we must heed God's written Word.

It is important to read and study the Bible because there is so much false teaching in the world. The Bible gives us the measuring stick by which we can distinguish truth from error. It tells us what God is like. To have a wrong impression of God is to worship an idol or false god. We are worshiping something that He is not. The Bible tells us how one truly gets to heaven (John 14:6; Ephesians 2:1–10; Isaiah 53:6; Romans 5:8; 6:23; 10:9–13). God's Word shows us just how much God loves us (Romans 5:6–8; John 3:16). And it is in learning this that we are drawn to love Him in return (1 John 4:19).

The Bible equips us to serve God (2 Timothy 3:17; Ephesians 6:17; Hebrews 4:12). Meditating on God's Word and obeying its teachings will bring success in life (Joshua 1:8; James 1:25). God's Word helps us see sin in our lives and helps us get rid of it (Psalm 119:9, 11). It supplies us with wisdom and guidance throughout our lives (Psalm 32:8; 119:99; Proverbs 1:6). The Bible keeps us from wasting years on that which does not matter and will not last (Matthew 7:24–27).

Reading and studying the Bible helps us see beyond the attractive "bait" of sinful temptations to the painful "hook." We can learn from others' mistakes rather than making them ourselves. There are so many Bible characters to learn from, some of whom can serve as both positive and negative role models. For example, David, in his defeat of Goliath, teaches us that God is greater than anything He asks us to face (1 Samuel 17), while his fall into adultery with Bathsheba reveals just how long-lasting and terrible the consequences of a moment's sinful pleasure can be (2 Samuel 11).

The Bible is a book that is not merely for reading. It is a book for studying, meditating on, and applying. It cannot be emphasized strongly enough just how important the Bible is to our lives.

Studying the Bible can be compared to mining for gold. If we put in little effort and merely sift through the pebbles in the stream, we will only find a little gold dust. But the more we really dig into it, the more reward we will have for our effort.

Question: What is bibliology?

Answer: Bibliology is the study of the Bible, the Word of God. The Bible is the inspired source of knowledge about God, Jesus Christ, salvation, and eternity. Without a proper understanding of the Bible, our views on these other issues become clouded and distorted. Bibliology tells us what the Bible is. Common questions in bibliology are:

1. **Is the Bible truly God's Word?** Our answer to this question does more than determine how we view the Bible and its importance in our lives; it will also have an eternal impact on us.

2. **What is the canon of Scripture?** The basis of Christianity is found in the authority of Scripture. If we can't identify what belongs in the Bible, then we can't properly distinguish theological truth from error.

3. **What does it mean that the Bible is inspired?** While there are different views as to what extent the Bible is inspired, there can be no doubt that the Bible itself claims that every word in every part of the Bible is inspired by God (1 Corinthians 2:12–13; 2 Timothy 3:16–17).

4. **Does the Bible contain errors, contradictions, or discrepancies?** The Bible is a coherent, consistent, and relatively easy-to-understand book. Bibliology brings the consistency to light and deals with critics' claims that the Bible contains errors.

5. **Is there proof for the inspiration of the Bible?** Among the proofs for the divine inspiration of the Bible are fulfilled prophecy, the unity of Scripture, and the support of archaeological findings. Inspiration's most important

proof, however, is the changed lives of those who read it, believe it, and live according to its precepts.

Bibliology teaches us that the Bible is inspired, meaning it is "breathed out" by God. Proper bibliology holds to the inerrancy of Scripture, meaning the Bible does not contain any errors, contradictions, or discrepancies. Solid bibliology helps us to understand how God used the personalities and styles of the human authors of Scripture and still produced His cohesive Word. Bibliology enables us to know why certain books were recognized as canonical while other books were excluded from the Bible.

For the Christian, the Bible is life itself. Its pages are filled with the very Spirit of God, revealing His heart and mind to us. What a wonderful and gracious God we have! He could have left us to struggle through life with no help at all, but He gave His Word to guide us, truly a "lamp to my feet and a light for my path" (Psalm 119:105).

Question: Where is a good place to start reading the Bible?

Answer: It is important to realize that the Bible is not an ordinary book that reads smoothly from cover to cover. It is actually a library, or collection, of books written by different authors in several languages over 1,500 years. Martin Luther said that the Bible is the "cradle of Christ," because all biblical history and prophecy ultimately point to Jesus. Therefore, any first reading of the Bible should probably begin with the Gospels. The gospel of Mark is quick and fast-paced and is a good place to start. Then you might want to go on to the gospel of John, which focuses on the things Jesus claimed about Himself. Mark tells about what Jesus did, while John tells about what Jesus said and who Jesus was. John contains some of the simplest and clearest passages, but also some of the deepest and most profound. Reading the Gospels (Matthew, Mark, Luke, and John) will familiarize you with Christ's life and ministry.

After that, read through some of the Epistles (Romans, Ephesians, or Philippians, for example). They teach us how to live our lives in a way that is honoring to God and give us some history on the early church. They also show us how to live in community with other Christians and how to share about our faith in Christ.

When you start reading the Old Testament, begin with the book of Genesis. It tells us how God created the world and how mankind fell into sin, as well as the impact that fall had on all of humanity. Exodus, Leviticus, Numbers, and Deuteronomy can be a bit hard to read, because they get into all the laws God required the Jews to live by under the Old Covenant. While you should not avoid these books, they are perhaps better left for later study.

Continue your reading with the book of Joshua through the Chronicles to get a good history of Israel. The Psalms, Proverbs, and Song of Solomon will give you a good feel for Hebrew poetry and wisdom. The prophetic books, Isaiah through Malachi, can be hard to grasp at times—but remember, the key to understanding the Bible is asking God for wisdom (James 1:5). God is the author of the Bible, and He wants you to understand His Word.

Not everyone can be a successful Bible student. Only those with the necessary "qualifications" for studying the Word can do so with God's blessings and the leading of the Holy Spirit. Before you dive into study, ask yourself the following:

1. Am I saved by faith in Jesus Christ (1 Corinthians 2:14–16)?
2. Am I hungering for God's Word (1 Peter 2:2)?
3. Am I committed to diligently searching God's Word (Acts 17:11)?

If you answered "yes" to these three questions, you can be sure that God will bless your efforts to know Him and His Word, no matter where you start and no matter what your method of study. If you are not a believer—meaning that you have not been saved by faith in Christ and do not have the Holy Spirit within you—you will find it impossible to understand the full meaning of the words of Scripture. Being born again is the place to start.

Question: What is the correct way to study the Bible?

Answer: Determining the meaning of Scripture is one of the most important tasks a believer has in this life. God does not tell us that we must simply read the Bible. We must study it and handle it correctly (2 Timothy 2:15). Studying the Scriptures is hard work. A cursory or brief scanning of Scripture can sometimes yield very wrong conclusions. Therefore, it is crucial to understand several principles for determining the correct meaning of Scripture.

First, the Bible student must pray and ask the Holy Spirit to impart understanding, for that is one of His functions. "But when he, the Spirit of truth, comes, he will guide you into all truth. He will not speak on his own; he will speak only what he hears, and he will tell you what is yet to come" (John 16:13). Just as the Holy Spirit guided the apostles in the writing of the New Testament, He also guides us in the understanding of Scripture (see 1 John 2:27). Remember, the Bible is God's book, and we need to ask Him what it means. If you are a Christian, the author of Scripture—the Holy Spirit—dwells inside you, and He wants you to understand what He wrote.

Second, we are not to pull a Scripture out of the verses that surround it and try to determine the meaning of the verse outside of the context. We should always read the surrounding verses and chapters to discern the context. While all of Scripture comes from God (2 Timothy 3:16), God used men to write it down (2 Peter 1:21). These men had a theme in mind, a purpose for writing, and a specific issue they were addressing. We should investigate the background of the book of the Bible we are studying to find out who wrote the book, to whom it was written, when it was written, and why it was written. Also, we should take care to let the text speak for itself. Sometimes people will assign their own meanings to words in order to get the interpretation they desire.

Third, we must not attempt to be totally independent in our study of the Bible. It is arrogant to think that we cannot gain understanding through the lifelong work of others who have studied Scripture. Some people, in error, approach the Bible with the idea that they will depend on the Holy Spirit alone and they will discover all the hidden truths of Scripture. The Holy Spirit has given spiritual gifts to every individual in the body of Christ. One of these spiritual gifts is that of teaching (Ephesians 4:11–12; 1 Corinthians 12:28). The Lord gives us these teachers to help us correctly understand and obey Scripture. It is always wise to study the Bible with other believers, assisting each other in understanding and applying the truth of God's Word.

So, in summary, what is the proper way to study the Bible? First, through prayer and humility, we must rely on the Holy Spirit to give us understanding. Second, we should always study Scripture in its context, recognizing that the Bible often explains itself. Third, we should respect the efforts of other Christians, past and present, who have also sought to properly study the Bible. Remember, God is the author of the Bible, and He wants us to understand it.

Question: What are some different methods of Bible study?

Answer: There are several different methods we can use to study the Bible in an organized or systematic way. For the purpose of this article, we will classify them into two broad categories: Book Studies and Topical Studies. Before discussing the different types of Bible study methods, it is important to recognize that all of them must follow certain hermeneutic rules or principles in order to avoid misinterpretations. For example, whatever type of Bible study method we use, it is important that the study carefully takes into consideration the context of the subject or verse being studied, both within the immediate context of the chapter or book itself and within the overall context of the Bible. Our first goal must be to understand what the original meaning of the passage is. In other words, what was the human author's intended meaning, and how would his original audience have understood what he wrote? This principle recognizes that the Bible was not written in a vacuum but is an historical document written at a specific point in history, with a specific audience in mind, and for a specific purpose. Once the true meaning of the passage is understood, we then should seek to understand how it applies to us today.

Book Studies

This method of Bible study focuses either on a complete book of the Bible or specific part of a book, such as a particular chapter, a range of verses, or a single verse. With chapter and verse-by-verse methods and with the study of an overall book, the principles and goals are the same. For example, in order to do a thorough book study, we must also study the context of individual chapters and verses. Likewise, in order to correctly study a particular verse, we need to also study the overall message of the chapter and book in which the verse is found. Of course, whether it is on the individual verse level or a complete book study, we must always consider the overall context of the whole Bible as well.

Topical Studies

There are many varieties of topical studies. Some examples include biographical studies, where we study all the Bible says about a particular person; word studies, where we study all the Bible says about a particular word or subject; and geographical studies, where we learn all we can about a particular town, country, or nation mentioned in the Bible. Topical studies are important for understanding all the Bible teaches on a particular subject or topic. We must be careful, though, that the conclusions drawn from a topical study do not come from taking verses out of their original context in order to imply a meaning that could not be supported with a verse study or book study. Topical studies are helpful in systematically organizing and understanding what the Bible teaches on specific subjects.

In studying the Bible, it is beneficial to use different methods at different times. Sometimes, we might want to devote extended time to do a book study, while at other times we can benefit greatly from doing a topical study. Whichever type of study we are doing, we can follow these basic steps:

1. **Observation:** What does the Bible say?
2. **Interpretation:** What does the Bible mean?
3. **Application:** How does this biblical truth apply to my life, or how is this passage relevant today?

No matter what method of Bible study we use, we must be careful to rightly divide the Word of God (2 Timothy 2:15).

Question: Why is it important to study the Bible in context? What is wrong with taking verses out of context?

Answer: It's important to study Bible passages and stories within their context. Taking verses out of context leads to all kinds of error and misinterpretation. Understanding context begins with four principles: literal meaning (what it says), historical setting (the events of the story, to whom it was addressed, and how it was understood at that time), grammar (the immediate sentence and paragraph within which a word or phrase is found), and synthesis (the comparison with other parts of Scripture). Context is crucial to biblical exegesis. After we account for the literal, historical, and grammatical nature of a passage, we must then focus on the structure of the book, then the chapter, then the paragraph. All of this is included in "context." To illustrate, it is like looking at a map of the world on Google Maps and gradually zooming in on one house.

Taking phrases and verses out of context almost always leads to misunderstanding. For instance, taking the phrase "God is love" (1 John 4:7–16) out of its context, we might think that our God loves everything and everyone at all times with a gushing, romantic type of love. But in its literal and grammatical context, "love" here refers to *agape* love, the essence of which is sacrifice for the benefit of another, not a sentimental or romantic feeling. The historical context is also crucial, because John was addressing believers in the first-century church and instructing them not on God's love per se, but on how to identify true believers from false professors. True love—the sacrificial, beneficial kind—is the mark of the true believer (verse 7); those who do not love do not belong to God (verse 8); God loved us before we loved Him (verses 9–10); and this is why we should love one another and thereby prove that we are His (verses 11–12).

Furthermore, considering the phrase "God is love" in the context of all of Scripture (synthesis) will keep us from coming to the false, and all-too-common, conclusion that God is *only* love or that His love is greater than all His other attributes. We know from many other passages that God is also holy and righteous, faithful and trustworthy, graceful and merciful, kind and compassionate, omnipotent, omnipresent, omniscient, and many other things. We also know from other passages that God not only loves, but He also hates (Psalm 11:5).

The Bible is the Word of God, literally "God-breathed" (2 Timothy 3:16), and we are commanded to read, study, and understand it through the use of good Bible study methods and always with the illumination of the Holy Spirit to guide us (1 Corinthians 2:14). Our study is greatly enhanced by maintaining diligence in the matter of context. It is not difficult to point out places that seemingly contradict other portions of Scripture, but if we carefully look at their context and use the entirety of Scripture as a reference, we can understand the meaning of a passage, and the apparent contradictions are explained. "Context is king" means that context often drives the meaning of a phrase. To ignore context is to put ourselves at a tremendous disadvantage.

Question: Why should we study the Old Testament?

Answer: There are many reasons to study the Old Testament. For one, the Old Testament lays the foundation for the teachings and events found in the New Testament. The Bible is a progressive revelation. If you skip the first half of any good book and try to finish it, you will have a hard time understanding the characters, the plot, and the ending. In the same way, the New Testament is only completely understood when we see its foundation of the events, characters, laws, sacrificial system, covenants, and promises of the Old Testament.

If we only had the New Testament, we would come to the Gospels and not know why the Jews were looking for a Messiah (a Savior King). We would not understand why this Messiah was coming (see Isaiah 53), and we would not have been able to identify Jesus of Nazareth as the Messiah through the many detailed prophecies that were given concerning Him [e.g., His birth place (Micah 5:2), His manner of death (Psalm 22, especially verses 1, 7–8, 14–18; 69:21), His resurrection (Psalm 16:10), and many more details of His ministry (Isaiah 9:2; 52:3)].

A study of the Old Testament is also important for understanding the Jewish customs mentioned in passing in the New Testament. We would not understand the way the Pharisees had perverted God's law by adding their own traditions to it, or why Jesus was so upset as He cleansed the temple courtyard, or where Jesus got the words He used in His many replies to adversaries.

The Old Testament records numerous detailed prophecies that could only have come true if the Bible is God's Word, not man's (e.g., Daniel 7 and the following chapters). Daniel's prophecies give specific details about the rise and fall of nations. These prophecies are so accurate, in fact, that skeptics choose to believe they were written after the fact.

We should study the Old Testament because of the countless lessons it contains for us. By observing the lives of the characters of the Old Testament, we find guidance for our own lives. We are exhorted to trust God no matter what (Daniel 3). We learn to stand firm in our convictions (Daniel 1) and to await the reward of faithfulness (Daniel 6). We learn it is best to confess sin early and sincerely instead of shifting blame (1 Samuel 15). We learn not to toy with sin, because it will find us out (Judges 13—16). We learn that our sin has consequences not only for ourselves but for our loved ones (Genesis 3) and, conversely, that our good behavior has rewards for us and those around us (Exodus 20:5–6).

A study of the Old Testament also helps us understand prophecy. The Old Testament contains many promises that God will yet fulfill for the Jewish nation. The Old Testament reveals such things as the length of the Tribulation, how Christ's future 1,000-year reign fulfills His promises to the Jews, and how the conclusion of the Bible ties up the loose ends that were unraveled in the beginning of time.

In summary, the Old Testament allows us to learn how to love and serve God, and it reveals more about God's character. It shows through repeatedly fulfilled prophecy why the Bible is unique among holy books. It is inspired Word of God. In short, if you have not yet ventured into the pages of the Old Testament, you are missing much of what God has available for you.

Question: What is good biblical exegesis?

Answer: *Exegesis* means "exposition or explanation." Biblical exegesis involves the examination of a particular text of Scripture in order to properly interpret it. Exegesis is a part of the process of hermeneutics, the science of interpretation. A person who practices exegesis is called an exegete.

Good biblical exegesis is actually commanded in Scripture. "Study [be diligent] to shew thyself approved unto God, a workman that needeth not to be ashamed, rightly dividing the word of truth" (2 Timothy 2:15 KJV). According to this verse, we must handle the Word of God properly, through diligent study. If we don't, we have reason to be ashamed.

There are some basic principles of good exegesis that serious students of the Bible will follow:

1. **The Grammatical Principle.** The Bible was written in human language, and language has a certain structure and follows certain rules. Therefore, we must interpret the Bible in a manner consistent with the basic rules of language.

   Usually, the exegete starts his examination of a passage by defining the words in it. Definitions are basic to understanding the passage as a whole, and it is important that the words be defined according to their original intent and not according to modern usage. To ensure accuracy, the exegete uses a precise English translation and Greek and Hebrew dictionaries.

Next, the exegete examines the syntax, or the grammatical relationships of the words in the passage. He finds parallels, he determines which ideas are primary and which are subordinate, and he discovers actions, subjects, and their modifiers. He may even diagram a verse or two.

2. **The Literal Principle.** We assume that each word in a passage has a normal, literal meaning, unless there is good reason to view it as a figure of speech. The exegete does not go out of his way to spiritualize or allegorize. Words mean what words mean.

So, if the Bible mentions a "horse," it means "a horse." When the Bible speaks of the Promised Land, it means a literal land given to Israel and should not be interpreted as a reference to heaven.

3. **The Historical Principle.** As time passes, culture changes, points of view change, language changes. We must guard against interpreting Scripture according to how our culture views things; we must always place Scripture in its historical context.

The diligent Bible student will consider the geography, the customs, the current events, and even the politics of the time when a passage was written. An understanding of ancient Jewish culture can greatly aid an understanding of Scripture. To do his research, the exegete will use Bible dictionaries, commentaries, and books on history.

4. **The Synthesis Principle.** The best interpreter of Scripture is Scripture itself. We must examine a passage in relation to its immediate context (the verses surrounding it), its wider context (the book it is found in), and its complete context (the Bible as a whole). The Bible does not contradict itself. Any theological statement in one verse can and should be harmonized with theological statements in other parts of

Scripture. Good Bible interpretation relates any one passage to the total content of Scripture.

5. **The Practical Principle.** Once we've properly examined the passage to understand its meaning, we have the responsibility to apply it to our own lives.

To "rightly divide the word of truth" through careful study and biblical exegesis is more than an intellectual exercise; it is a life-changing event.

Question: What is the difference between exegesis and eisegesis?

Answer: Exegesis and eisegesis are two conflicting approaches in Bible study. Exegesis is the exposition or explanation of a text based on a careful, objective analysis. The word *exegesis* literally means "to lead out of." That means that the interpreter is led to his conclusions by following the text.

The opposite approach to Scripture is eisegesis, which is the interpretation of a passage based on a subjective, non-analytical reading. The word *eisegesis* literally means "to lead into," which means the interpreter injects his own ideas into the text, making it mean whatever he wants.

Obviously, only exegesis does justice to the text. Eisegesis is a mishandling of the text and often leads to a misinterpretation. Exegesis is concerned with discovering the true meaning of the text, respecting its grammar, syntax, and setting. Eisegesis is concerned only with making a point, even at the expense of the meaning of words.

Second Timothy 2:15 commands us to use exegetical methods: "Do your best to present yourself to God as one approved, a workman who does not need to be ashamed and who correctly handles the word of truth." An honest student of the Bible will be an exegete, allowing the text to speak for itself. Eisegesis easily lends itself to error, as the would-be interpreter attempts to align the text with his own preconceived notions. Exegesis allows us to agree with the Bible; eisegesis seeks to force the Bible to agree with us.

The process of exegesis involves 1) observation: what does the passage say?, 2) interpretation: what does the passage mean?, 3) correlation: how does the passage relate to the rest of the Bible?, and 4) application: how should this passage affect my life?

Eisegesis, on the other hand, involves 1) imagination: what idea do I want to present?, 2) exploration: what Scripture passage seems to fit with my idea?, and 3) application: what does my idea mean? Notice that, in eisegesis, there is no examination of the words of the text or their relationship to each other, no cross-referencing with related passages, and no real desire to understand the actual meaning. Scripture serves only as a prop to the interpreter's idea.

To illustrate, let's use both approaches in the treatment of one passage.

2 Chronicles 27:1–2
"Jotham was twenty-five years old when he became king, and he reigned in Jerusalem sixteen years. . . . He did what was right in the eyes of the Lord, just as his father Uzziah had done, but unlike him he did not enter the temple of the Lord."

Eisegesis

First, the interpreter decides on a topic. Today, it's "The Importance of Church Attendance." The interpreter reads 2 Chronicles 27:1–2 and sees that King Jotham was a good king, just like his father Uzziah had been, except for one thing: he didn't go to the temple! This passage seems to fit the interpreter's idea, so he uses it. The resulting sermon deals with the need for passing on godly values from one generation to the next. Just because King Uzziah went to the temple every week didn't mean that his son would continue the practice. In the same way, many young people today tragically turn from their parents' training, and church attendance drops off. The sermon ends with a question: "How many blessings did Jotham fail to receive simply because he neglected church?"

Certainly, there is nothing wrong with preaching about church attendance or the transmission of values. And a cursory reading of 2 Chronicles 27:1–2 seems to support that passage as an apt illustration. However, the above interpretation is totally wrong. For Jotham not to go to the temple was not wrong; in fact, it was very good, as the proper approach to the passage will show.

Exegesis

First, the interpreter reads the passage and, to fully understand the context, he reads the histories of both Uzziah and Jotham (2 Chronicles 26—27; 2 Kings 15:1–6, 32–38). In his observation, he discovers that King Uzziah was a good king who nevertheless disobeyed the Lord when he went to the temple and offered incense on the altar—something only a priest had the right to do (2 Chronicles 26:16–20). Uzziah's pride and his contamination of the temple resulted in his having "leprosy until the day he died" (2 Chronicles 26:21).

Needing to know why Uzziah spent the rest of his life in isolation, the interpreter studies Leviticus 13:46 and does some research on leprosy. Then he compares the use of illness as a punishment in other passages, such as 2 Kings 5:27 and 21:12–15.

By this time, the exegete understands something important: when the passage says Jotham "did not enter the temple of the LORD," it means he did not repeat his father's mistake. Uzziah had proudly usurped the priest's office; Jotham was more obedient.

The resulting sermon might deal with the Lord's discipline of His children, with the blessing of total obedience, or with our need to learn from the mistakes of the past rather than repeat them.

Of course, exegesis takes more time than eisegesis. But, if we are to be those unashamed workmen "who correctly handle the word of truth," then we must take the time to truly understand the text. Exegesis is the only way.

Question: What is biblical hermeneutics?

Answer: Biblical hermeneutics is the science of properly interpreting Scripture. Hermeneutics involves identifying the type of literature a passage is written in, conducting the exegesis of the passage, and drawing conclusions based on what the passage says. The purpose of biblical hermeneutics is to help us to know how to interpret, understand, and apply the Bible.

The most important law of biblical hermeneutics is that the Bible should be interpreted literally. Literal Bible interpretation means we understand the Bible in its normal or plain meaning. The Bible says what it means and means what it says. Many make the mistake of trying to read between the lines and come up with meanings for Scriptures that are not truly in the text. Yes, of course, there are some spiritual truths behind the plain meanings of Scripture. But that does not mean that every Scripture has a hidden spiritual truth, or that it should be our goal to find all such esoteric truths. Biblical hermeneutics keeps us faithful to the intended meaning of Scripture and away from allegorizing and symbolizing Bible verses and passages that should be understood literally.

A second crucial law of biblical hermeneutics is that a verse or passage must be interpreted historically, grammatically, and contextually. Historical interpretation refers to understanding the culture, background, and situation that prompted the writing of the text. Grammatical interpretation is recognizing the rules of the grammar and the nuances of the Hebrew and Greek languages and using those rules to understand a passage. Contextual interpretation involves taking the surrounding context of a passage into consideration when trying to determine the meaning.

Some mistakenly view biblical hermeneutics as limiting our ability to learn new truths from God's Word or stifling the Holy Spirit's ability to reveal to us its meaning. This is not the case. The goal of biblical hermeneutics is to point us to the correct interpretation of a text, to understand the Holy Spirit's inspired message. The purpose of biblical hermeneutics is to guide us to a proper understanding of a passage and protect us from improperly applying it. Biblical hermeneutics points us to the true meaning and application of Scripture.

Hebrews 4:12 declares, "For the word of God is living and active. Sharper than any double-edged sword, it penetrates even to dividing soul and spirit, joints and marrow; it judges the thoughts and attitudes of the heart." The principles of hermeneutics train us to skillfully wield the sword.

Question: Is it important to know Greek and Hebrew when studying the Bible?

Answer: Martin Luther, the great Protestant Reformer, wrote the following in regard to the importance of understanding Greek and Hebrew when studying the Scriptures: "The languages are the sheath in which the sword of the Spirit is contained." God sovereignly chose to have His Word written in Hebrew (the Old Testament) and Greek (the New Testament).

Our modern English translations are excellent. Most of the major English translations available today are superb renderings of the original Greek and Hebrew. However, in any translation, not everything that was communicated in the original language can be precisely conveyed in another language. Some nuances do not transfer well from one language to another. As a result, a translation is rarely, if ever, a perfect rendering of the original. (This is one reason why the Amplified Version was published.)

An example of this is the "aspect" of Greek verbs. English verbs have tenses—past, present, and future. Greek verbs have these same tenses, but they also have what is known as "aspect." Present-tense Greek verbs mean more than the action is occurring presently. A Greek verb can also carry the meaning that the action is occurring continually or repeatedly. This is lost in English unless the aspect word "continually" or "repeatedly" is added to the translation along with the verb. A specific example of this is Ephesians 5:18, "... be filled with the Spirit." In the original Greek, this verse is telling us to continually be filled with the Spirit. It is not a one-time event—it is a lifelong process. This "aspect" is lost in the English translation.

With all that said, the Bible also makes it clear that the Spirit is the author of the Bible and that He will help us to understand His Word (2 Timothy 3:16–17). You do not have to know Hebrew and Greek in order to understand the Bible. God's intended message for us is accurately communicated in English. You can have confidence that God can reveal the meaning of His Word to you without your knowing Greek and Hebrew.

Perhaps this is a good analogy: reading the Bible without knowing Greek and Hebrew is like watching a 42-inch television, while reading the Bible knowing Greek and Hebrew is like watching a 65-inch LED 1080p HDTV with stereo surround sound. You can understand what is going on with the 42-inch television, but the 65-inch LED 1080p HDTV with stereo surround sound gives added depth and clarity. With the help of the Holy Spirit, anyone can accurately understand the Bible in English. However, knowing Hebrew and Greek helps to better understand the nuances and richness of the biblical texts.

Question: What are the different forms of biblical literature?

Answer: One of the most intriguing facts about the Bible is that, while it is God's communication to us, human beings were part of the writing process. As Hebrews 1:1 says, "In the past God spoke to our forefathers through the prophets at many times and in various ways." The "various ways" include different literary genres. The Bible's human writers used different forms of literature to communicate different messages at different times.

The Bible contains historical literature (1 and 2 Kings), dramatic literature (Job), legal documents (much of Exodus and Deuteronomy), song lyrics (The Song of Solomon and Psalms), poetry (most of Isaiah), wisdom literature (Proverbs and Ecclesiastes), apocalyptic literature (Revelation and parts of Daniel), short story (Ruth), sermons (as recorded in Acts), speeches and proclamations (like those of King Nebuchadnezzar in Daniel), prayers (many Psalms), parables (such as those Jesus told), fables (such as Jotham told), and epistles (Ephesians and Romans).

The different genres can overlap. Many of the psalms, for example, are both prayers and song lyrics. Some of the epistles contain poetry. Each type of literature has unique characteristics that should be approached with due consideration. For example, Jotham's fable (Judges 9:7–15) cannot be interpreted the same way as the Ten Commandments (Exodus 20:1–17). Interpreting poetry, with its reliance on metaphor and other poetic devices, is different from interpreting historical narrative.

Second Peter 1:21 says that "men spoke from God as they were carried along by the Holy Spirit." Using today's terminology, the Bible's managing editor was the Holy Spirit of God. God put the mark of His authorship on each of the 66 books of the Bible, no matter what the literary genre. God "breathed" the written words (2 Timothy 3:16). Because mankind has the ability to understand and appreciate various forms of literature, God used many genres to communicate His Word. The reader of the Bible will discover a common purpose that unifies the parts of the collection. He will discover motifs, foreshadowing, repeated themes, and recurring characters. Through it all, he will find that the Bible is the world's greatest literary masterpiece—and the very Word of God.

Question: How should the different genres of the Bible impact how we interpret the Bible?

Answer: The Bible is a work of literature. Literature comes in different genres, or categories based on style, and each is read and appreciated differently from another. For example, to confuse a work of science fiction with a medical textbook would cause many problems—they must be understood differently. And both science fiction and a medical text must be understood differently from poetry. Therefore, accurate interpretation takes into consideration the purpose and style of a given book or passage of Scripture. An inability to identify genre can lead to serious misunderstanding of Scripture.

The main genres found in the Bible are these: law, history, wisdom, poetry, narrative, epistles, prophecy, and apocalyptic literature. The summary below shows the differences between each genre and how each should be interpreted.

1. **Law**: This includes the books of Leviticus and Deuteronomy. The purpose of law is to express God's sovereign will concerning government, priestly duties, social responsibilities, etc. Knowledge of Hebrew manners and customs of the time, as well as familiarity with the covenants, will complement a reading of this material.

2. **History**: Stories and epics from the Bible are included in this genre. Almost every book in the Bible contains some history, but Genesis, Exodus, Numbers, Joshua, Judges, 1 and 2 Samuel, 1 and 2 Kings, 1 and 2 Chronicles, Ezra, Nehemiah, and Acts are predominately history. Knowledge of secular history is crucial, as it dovetails perfectly with biblical history and makes interpretation much more robust.

3. **Wisdom**: This is the genre of aphorisms that teach the meaning of life and how to live. Some of the language used in wisdom literature is metaphorical and poetic, and this should be taken into account during analysis. Included are the books of Proverbs, Job, and Ecclesiastes.

4. **Poetry**: These include books of rhythmic prose, parallelism, and metaphor, such as Song of Solomon, Lamentations, and Psalms. We know that David, himself a musician, and David's worship leader, Asaph, wrote many of the psalms. Because poetry does not translate easily, we lose some of the musical "flow" in English. Nevertheless, we find a similar use of idiom, comparison, and refrain in this genre as we find in modern music.

5. **Narrative**: This genre includes the Gospels, which are biographical narratives about Jesus, and the books of

Ruth, Esther, and Jonah. A reader may find bits of other genres within the Gospels, such as parable (Luke 8:1–15, for example) and discourse (see Matthew 24). The book of Ruth is a perfect model of a well-crafted short story, amazing in its succinctness and structure.

6. **Epistles:** An epistle is a letter, usually in a formal style. There are 21 letters in the New Testament from the apostles to various churches or individuals. These letters have a style very similar to modern letters, with an opening, a greeting, a body, and a closing. The content of the Epistles involves clarification of prior teaching, rebuke, explanation, correction of false teaching, and a deeper look into the teachings of Jesus. The reader would do well to understand the cultural, historical, and social situation of the original recipients in order to get the most out of an analysis of these books.

7. **Prophecy and Apocalyptic Literature:** The prophetic writings are the Old Testament books of Isaiah through Malachi, as well as the New Testament book of Revelation. They include predictions of future events, warnings of coming judgment, and an overview of God's plan for Israel. Apocalyptic literature is a specific form of prophecy, largely involving symbols and imagery and predicting disaster and destruction. We find this type of language in Daniel (the beasts of chapter 7), Ezekiel (the scroll of chapter 3), Zechariah (the golden lampstand of chapter 4), and Revelation (the four horsemen of chapter 6). The prophetic and apocalyptic books are the ones most often subjected to faulty exegesis and personal interpretation based on emotion or preconceived bias. However, Amos 3:7 tells us, "Surely the Sovereign LORD does nothing without revealing his plan to his servants the prophets." Therefore, we know that the truth has been told, and much of it can be known via careful exegesis, a familiarity with the rest of the Bible, and prayerful consideration. Some things will not be made clear to us except in the fullness of time, so it is best not

to assume to know everything when it comes to prophetic literature.

An understanding of the genres of Scripture is vital to the Bible student. If the wrong genre is assumed for a passage, the text can easily be misunderstood or misconstrued, leading to an incomplete and fallacious understanding of what God desires to communicate. God is not the author of confusion (1 Corinthians 14:33), and He wants us to "correctly [handle] the word of truth" (2 Timothy 2:15). In addition, God wants us to know His plan for the world and for us as individuals. How fulfilling it is to come to "grasp how wide and long and high and deep" (Ephesians 3:18) is the love of God for us!

Question: Does the Bible contain allegory?

Answer: An allegory is a story in which the characters and/or events are symbols representing other events, ideas, or people. Allegory has been a common literary device throughout the history of literature. Allegories have been used to indirectly express unpopular or controversial ideas, to critique politics, and to rebuke those in power (e.g., George Orwell's *Animal Farm* and Jonathan Swift's *Gulliver's Travels*). Other times, allegory is used to express abstract ideas or spiritual truths through an extended metaphor, making the truth easier to grasp (e.g., John Bunyan's *The Pilgrim's Progress* and Hannah Hurnard's *Hinds' Feet on High Places*).

The Bible contains many instances of allegory used to explain spiritual truths or to foreshadow later events. The clearest examples of allegory in Scripture are the parables of Jesus. In these stories, the characters and events represent a truth about the kingdom of God or the Christian life. For example, in the parable of the sower in Matthew 13:3–9, the seed and different types of soil illustrate the Word of God and various responses to it (as Jesus explains in verses 18–23).

The story of the prodigal son also makes use of allegory. In this story (Luke 15:11–32), the son represents the average person: sinful and prone to selfishness. The wealthy father represents God, and the son's harsh life of hedonism and subsequent poverty represents the hollowness of the ungodly lifestyle. When the son returns home in genuine sorrow, we have an illustration of repentance. In the father's mercy and willingness to receive his son back, we see God's joy when we turn from sin and seek His forgiveness.

In the parables, Jesus teaches abstract spiritual concepts (how people react to the gospel, God's mercy, etc.) in the form of relatable metaphors. We gain a deeper understanding of God's truth through these stories. Other examples of biblical allegory, as a literary form, include the vision of the dragon and the woman in Revelation 12:1–6; the story of the eagles and the vine in Ezekiel 17; and many of the proverbs, especially those written in emblematic parallelism.

Some of the traditions and ceremonies instituted by God in the Bible could be considered non-literary allegories because they symbolize spiritual truths. The act of animal sacrifice, for example, represented that our sins deserve death, and each substitute on the altar prefigured the eventual sacrifice of Christ, who would die for His people. The institution of marriage, while serving great practical purposes, is also a symbol of the relationship between Christ and the Church (Ephesians 5:31–32). Many of the ceremonial laws of Moses (regarding clothing, foods, and clean and unclean objects) represented spiritual realities such as the need for believers to be distinct in spirit and action from non-believers. While these examples may not be considered allegories individually (since an allegory requires multiple symbols working together), the religious system of the Old Testament (and parts of the New) can be seen as a broad allegory for man's relationship with God.

Interestingly, some significant historical events, which appear at first glance to contain no deeper meaning, are interpreted allegorically later to teach an important lesson. One instance of this is Galatians 4, where Paul interprets the story of Abraham, Hagar, and Sarah as an allegory for the Old and New Covenants. He writes, "For it is written that Abraham had two sons, one by the slave woman and the other by the free woman. His son by the slave woman was born in the ordinary way; but his son by the free woman was born as the result of a promise. These things may be taken figuratively, for the women represent two covenants. One covenant is from Mount Sinai and bears children who are to be slaves: This is Hagar. Now Hagar stands for Mount Sinai in Arabia and corresponds to the present city of Jerusalem, because she is in slavery with her children. But the Jerusalem that is above is free, and she is our mother" (Galatians 4:22–26). Here, Paul takes actual, historical people (Abraham, Hagar, and Sarah) and uses them as symbols for the law of Moses (the Old Covenant) and the freedom of Christ (the New Covenant). Through Paul's allegorical lens, we see that our relationship with God is one of freedom (we are children of the divine promise, as Isaac was to Sarah), not of bondage (we are not children of man's bondage, as Ishmael was to Hagar). Paul, through the inspiration of the Holy Spirit, could see the symbolic significance of this historical event and used it to illustrate our position in Christ.

Allegory is a beautifully artistic way of explaining spiritual matters in easily understood terms. Through the Bible's allegories, God helps us understand difficult concepts in a more relatable context. He also reveals Himself as the Great Storyteller, working through history to foreshadow and carry out His plan. We can rejoice that we have a God who addresses us in ways we can understand and who has given us symbols and allegories to remind us of Himself.

Question: What is biblical typology?

Answer: Typology is a special kind of symbolism. (A symbol is something that represents something else.) We can define a type as a "prophetic symbol," because all types are representations of something in the future. More specifically, a "type" in Scripture is an Old Testament person or thing that foreshadows a person or thing in the New Testament. For example, the flood of Noah's day (Genesis 6—8) is used as a type of baptism in 1 Peter 3:20–21.

When we say that someone is a type of Christ, we are saying that a person in the Old Testament behaves in a way that corresponds to Jesus' character or actions in the New Testament. When we say that something is "typical" of Christ, we are saying that an object or event in the Old Testament can be viewed as representative of some quality of Jesus.

Scripture itself identifies several Old Testament events as types of Christ's redemption, including the tabernacle, the sacrificial system, and the Passover. The Old Testament tabernacle is identified as a type in Hebrews 9:8–9: "The first tabernacle … was a figure for the time then present" (KJV). The high priest's entrance into the holiest place once a year typified the mediation of Christ, our High Priest. Later, the veil of the tabernacle is said to be a type of Christ (Hebrews 10:19–20) in that His flesh was torn (as the veil was when He was crucified) in order to provide entrance into God's presence for those who are covered by His sacrifice.

The whole sacrificial system is seen as a type in Hebrews 9:18–26. The articles of the "first covenant" were dedicated with the blood of sacrifice; these articles are called "the copies of the heavenly things" and "a copy of the true" (verses 23–24). This passage teaches that the Old Testament sacrifices typify Christ's final sacrifice for the sins of the world. The Passover is also a type of Christ, according to 1 Corinthians 5:7, "Christ our passover is sacrificed for us" (KJV). Discovering exactly what the events of the Passover teach us about Christ is a rich and rewarding study.

We should point out the difference between an illustration and a type. A type is always identified as such in the New Testament. A Bible student finding correlations between an Old Testament story and the life of Christ is simply finding illustrations, not types. In other words, Scripture determines typology. The Holy Spirit inspired the use of types; illustrations and analogies are the result of man's study. For example, many people see parallels between Joseph (Genesis 37—45) and Jesus. The humiliation and subsequent glorification of Joseph seem to correspond to the death and resurrection of Christ. However, the New Testament never uses Joseph as a model of Christ; therefore, Joseph's story is properly called an illustration, but not a type, of Christ.

Question: Is there any validity to Bible codes?

Answer: Many people claim to have discovered amazing patterns using some sort of Bible code. There are some Bible code results that seem to reveal specific information. We cannot completely rule out the possibility that God could have "hidden" information in His Word. However, since we know that God wants us to understand His Word (2 Timothy 3:16–17), we must ask ourselves why He would "hide" valuable information in His Word that would be impossible for people to discover for thousands of years? This flies in the face of what we know about God's character and purpose. Would a good and merciful God hide the very information we need to understand good and evil, heaven and hell, and sin and redemption, and then hold us accountable for all eternity because we failed to act upon that information? Of course He would not.

Aside from the attack on God's character, the main problem with Bible codes is that they do not fit with proper biblical interpretation. Jesus, in all His citations of Bible passages, never once used a "Bible code" to decipher a meaning. In all the times the apostle Paul references Old Testament passages, he never once uses a "Bible code" to arrive at an interpretation. The same could be said for all of the other biblical authors who reference other books of the Bible. We are never instructed by any Bible passage to look for Bible codes to determine its meaning (or to gain any deeper insight). What we need to know and apply is clear enough from a straight reading of the Word of God.

"Faith comes from hearing the message, and the message is heard through the word of Christ" (Romans 10:17). And the message is simple. Faith is not the result of discovering hidden codes or deciphering esoteric messages. Passages such as Psalm 119:9–11, 105; 2 Timothy 3:16–17; and 1 Peter 2:2 all refer to taking the text of God's Word at face value and applying its principles to our lives. Obedience to the plain Word of God is required, not the seeking out of alphanumeric codes.

Finally, the codes are arbitrary both as to how they are "discovered" and how they are interpreted. But again, the main argument against the use of Bible codes is that they are simply unbiblical and thus invalid. All we need from the Bible is found in the existing text (2 Timothy 2:15; 3:16–17).

Question: What is the biblical doctrine of illumination?

Answer: Simply put, illumination in the spiritual sense is "turning on the light" of understanding in some area. God gives enlightenment, and Jesus is the "true light" (John 1:9). When the enlightenment deals with new knowledge or future things, we call it prophecy. When the enlightenment deals with understanding and applying knowledge already given, we call it illumination.

Illumination is the Spirit's work in a believer's heart to truly understand the Scriptures. The Holy Spirit wrote the Bible through the process of inspiration. He helps us understand the Bible through the process of illumination. Without the Spirit's illuminating work in our hearts, we cannot understand the Word properly (1 Corinthians 2:14; Ephesians 4:18). The Holy Spirit causes us to "understand what God has freely given us" (1 Corinthians 2:12), as He teaches us (1 John 2:27).

The purpose of God's illumination is more than just an accurate understanding of God's Word. Such an understanding can be quite academic and impractical, and, as we know, "knowledge puffs up" (1 Corinthians 8:1). There is no question that God desires us to accurately understand His Word. But we must go on to be doers of the Word (James 1:22). The Spirit's illumination of His Word should change our lives.

Psalm 119, the longest chapter in the Bible, is a song about God's Word. Verse 130 says, "The unfolding of your words gives light; it gives understanding to the simple." This verse reveals the basic method of God's illumination—His Word. When God's Word enters the heart of a person, it gives "light" and understanding to him. For this reason, we are repeatedly told to study the Word of God. Regular study of the Word of God will give direction and understanding in the issues of life.

God's illumination is requested in Psalm 119:18: "Open my eyes that I may see wonderful things in your law." God's law had been around for a long time, and the writer asks for understanding as he studies the law—he wants one of those "aha!" moments. Similarly, verse 73 says, "Your hands made me and formed me; give me understanding to learn your commands." The writer's plea is for personal understanding and application of God's laws. In Psalm 119 the writer asks God 15 times to teach or give understanding regarding His laws.

Ephesians 1:17–18 tells us that the Spirit gives wisdom and revelation concerning Jesus Christ and opens the eyes of understanding so we can know God's purposes in our lives. In 1 Corinthians 2:9–13, we see that God has revealed His plans for us by His Spirit, who teaches us spiritual things. The context here points to the Word of God as that which has been revealed. The Spirit of God will always point us to the Word of God for our instruction. The Bible is the Spirit's sword (Ephesians 6:17). As Jesus told His disciples in John 16:12–15, the Spirit simply repeats what the Father and the Son have already said. This repetition helps us remember and fully hear what God has already told us. Sometimes we have to hear things several times before we actually *listen* to them. That's where the Spirit comes in.

Going back to Psalm 119, we find a determination to take action connected with the illumination verses: "I will meditate on your wonders" (verse 27), "I will keep your law and obey it with all my heart" (verse 34). We also find purpose statements: "that I may understand your statutes" (verse 125), "that I may live" (verse 144). The illumination always points to action.

God gave us His Word and helps us to understand it. We are then able to live in its light. First John 1:6 challenges us, "If we claim to have fellowship with him yet walk in the darkness, we lie and do not live by the truth." We could paraphrase it to say, "If we say we've been enlightened, but still walk in the dark, we lie about understanding God's Word." The Spirit of God, who enlightens us to hear and understand His Word, then takes that knowledge and guides us in living it. "For as many as are led by the Spirit of God, they are the sons of God" (Romans 8:14). The guidance and illumination of the Holy Spirit are confirmations that we are indeed children of God.

Chapter 8

QUESTIONS ABOUT APPLYING THE BIBLE

Contents

Question: Is the Bible relevant for today?

Answer: Hebrews 4:12 says, "For the word of God is living and active. Sharper than any double-edged sword, it penetrates even to dividing soul and spirit, joints and marrow; it judges the thoughts and attitudes of the heart." While the Bible was completed approximately 1,900 years ago, its "sharpness" and relevance for today remain unchanged. God has not changed, human nature has not changed, and the Bible still speaks from God to the world. The Bible is the sole objective source of all the revelation of God about Himself and His plan for humanity.

The Bible contains a great deal of information about the natural world that has been confirmed by scientific observations and research. Some of these passages include Leviticus 17:11; Ecclesiastes 1:6–7; Job 36:27–29; Psalm 102:25–27; and Colossians 1:16-17. As the Bible's story of God's redemptive plan for humanity unfolds, many different characters are vividly described. In those descriptions, the Bible provides a great deal of information about human behavior and tendencies. Our own day-to-day experience shows us that this information is more accurate and descriptive of the human condition than any psychology textbook. Many historical facts recorded in the Bible have been confirmed by extra-biblical sources. Historical research often shows a great deal of agreement between biblical accounts and extra-biblical accounts of the same events.

However, the Bible is not a history book, a psychology text, or a scientific journal. The Bible is the description God gave us about who He is and His desires and plans for humanity. The most significant component of this revelation is the story of our separation from God by sin and God's provision for restoration of fellowship through the sacrifice of His Son, Jesus Christ, on the cross. Our need for redemption does not change. Neither does God's desire to reconcile us to Himself.

All Scripture is profitable (2 Timothy 3:16). The Bible's most important message—redemption—is universally and perpetually applicable to humanity. God's Word will never be outdated, superseded, or improved upon. Cultures change, laws change, generations come and go, but the Word of God is as relevant today as when it was first written. Not all of Scripture necessarily applies *explicitly* to us today, but every passage contains *implicit* principles that we can, and should, apply to our lives today.

Question: How can we know what parts of the Bible apply to us today?

Answer: Much misunderstanding occurs when we assign commands we should follow as "era-specific" (only applying to the original audience), or when we mistake commands specific to a particular audience as timeless truths. How do we discern the difference? The first thing to note is that the canon of Scripture was closed by the end of the first century AD. What that means is most, if not all, of the Bible was not originally written to us. The authors had in mind the hearers of that day and probably were not aware that their words would be read by people all over the world centuries later. That should cause us to be very careful when interpreting the Bible for today's Christian. It seems that much of contemporary preaching is so concerned with relevance that we treat the Bible as a lake from which to fish application for today's Christians. This is done at the expense of proper exegesis and interpretation.

The top three rules of hermeneutics (the art and science of biblical interpretation) are 1) context, 2) context, and 3) context. Before we can tell 21st-century Christians how the Bible applies to them, we must first come to the best possible understanding of what the Bible meant to its original audience. If we come up with an application that would have been foreign to the original audience, there is a strong possibility that we did not interpret the passage correctly. Once we are confident that we understand what the text meant to its original hearers, we then need to consider the dissimilarities between them and us. What are the differences in language, time, culture, geography, setting, and situation? All of these must be taken into account before an application can be made. Once we understand the divergence of our cultures, we can find commonalities between the original audience and ourselves. Finally, we can find application for ourselves in our time and situation.

Also important is the fact that each passage has only one correct interpretation. It can have a range of application, but only one interpretation. This means that some applications are better than others. If one application is closer to the correct interpretation than another, then it is a better application of that text. For example, many sermons have been preached on 1 Samuel 17 (the David and Goliath story) that involve "defeating the giants in your life." They lightly skim the details of the narrative and go straight to application, which usually involves allegorizing Goliath into a difficult, intimidating situation that must be overcome by faith. There are also attempts to allegorize the five smooth stones David picked up. These sermons usually conclude by exhorting us to be faithful like David.

While these interpretations make engaging sermons, it is doubtful the original audience would have gotten that message from this story. Before we can apply the truth of 1 Samuel 17, we must know how the original audience understood it, and that means determining the overall purpose of 1 Samuel as a book. Without going into a detailed exegesis, let's just say it's not about defeating the giants in your life. That may be a distant *application* of the passage, but as an *interpretation*, it's alien to the text. God is the hero of the story, and David is His chosen vehicle to bring salvation to His people. The story contrasts the people's king (Saul) with God's king (David), and it also foreshadows what Christ (the Son of David) would do in providing our salvation.

Another example of interpreting without regard to the context is found in many sermons on John 14:13–14. Reading these verses out of context could cause someone to conclude that if we ask God *anything,* we will receive it as long as we use the formula "in Jesus' name." Applying the rules of proper hermeneutics to this passage, we see Jesus speaking to His disciples in the upper room on the night of His betrayal. The immediate audience is the disciples. This is essentially a promise to Jesus' disciples that God will provide the necessary resources for them to complete their task. It is a passage of comfort because Jesus would soon be leaving them. Is there an application for 21st-century Christians? Of course! If we

150

pray according to God's will (in Jesus' name), God will give us what we need to accomplish His plans in and through us. Furthermore, the response we get will always glorify God. Far from promising that God will give us whatever we want, this passage teaches us to submit to God's will in prayer and that God will always provide what we need to accomplish His will.

Proper biblical interpretation is built on the following principles:

1. Start small and extend outward to understand the context: verse, passage, chapter, book, author, and testament/ covenant.
2. Ascertain how the original audience would have understood the text.
3. Think through the differences between your culture and that of the original audience.
4. Consider any moral command from the Old Testament that is repeated in the New Testament as a "timeless truth."
5. Remember that each passage has only one correct interpretation but can have many applications (some better than others).
6. Be humble and don't forget the role of the Holy Spirit in interpretation. He has promised to lead us into all truth (1 John 2:27).

Biblical interpretation is as much an art as it is a science. There are rules to follow, and some of the more difficult passages require more effort than others. We should always be open to changing an interpretation if the Spirit convicts and the evidence supports.

Question: What is the key to applying the Bible to my life?

Answer: Applying the Bible is the duty of all Christians. If we don't apply it, the Bible becomes nothing more to us than a dry, tedious tome, an impractical collection of old manuscripts. That's why Paul says, "Whatever you have learned or received or heard from me, or seen in me—put it into practice. And the God of peace will be with you" (Philippians 4:9). When we apply the Bible, God Himself will be with us.

The first step toward applying God's Word in our lives is reading it. There are hundreds of Bible reading plans available on the Internet and through various Christian ministries that we can use to familiarize ourselves with God's Word. Our goal in reading is to get to know God, to learn His ways, and to understand His purpose for this world and for us individually. In reading the Bible, we will learn about God's interactions with humanity throughout history, His plan of redemption, His promises, and His character. We will see what the Christian life looks like. The knowledge of God we glean from Scripture serves as an invaluable foundation for applying the Bible's principles for life.

Our next goal is what the psalmist refers to as "hiding" God's Word in our hearts: "I have hidden your word in my heart that I might not sin against you" (Psalm 119:11). The way we "hide" God's Word in our hearts is by studying, memorizing, and meditating on what we have first read. These four steps—read, study, memorize, and meditate—make it possible to successfully apply the Scriptures to our lives.

Study: While studying certainly involves reading, reading is not the same as studying. To study God's Word means that we prayerfully devote time and attention to acquiring advanced knowledge of a particular person, subject, theme, passage, or book of the Bible. Many study resources are available online, as well as commentaries or published Bible studies that enable us to get into the "meat" of God's Word (Hebrews 5:13–14). We can familiarize ourselves with these resources, then choose a topic, passage, or book that piques our interest, and delve in.

Memorize: It is impossible to apply what we cannot remember. If we are going to "hide" the Word in our hearts, we have to first get it in there by means of memorization. Memorizing Scripture produces within us a well from which we may continually drink, especially at times when we are not able to read our Bibles. In the same way that we store up money and other earthly possessions for future use, we should "fix these words of mine in your hearts and minds" (Deuteronomy 11:18). We should create a plan for the Scripture verses we would like to memorize each week.

Meditate: We must reflect on what we read in the Bible in order to properly apply it to our lives. In the parable of the four soils (Matthew 13:3–9; cf. 18–23), Jesus tells of a sower who goes out to sow seed in his field, but some of the seed—the Word of God (Matthew 13:19)—falls on "rocky places, where it did not have much soil. It sprang up quickly, because the soil was shallow. But when the sun came up, the plants were scorched, and they withered because they had no root" (13:5–6). This, Jesus says, is the person in whom the Word is sown but does not take root (13:20–21).

Psalm 1:1–2 says that the man who meditates on God's Word is blessed. Donald S. Whitney, in his classic work *Spiritual Disciplines for the Christian Life*, writes, "The tree of your spiritual life thrives best with meditation because it helps you absorb the water of God's Word (Ephesians 5:26). Merely hearing or reading the Bible, for example, can be like a short rainfall on hard ground. Regardless of the amount or intensity of the rain, most runs off and little sinks in. Meditation opens the soil of the soul and lets the water of God's Word percolate in deeply. The result is an extraordinary fruitfulness and spiritual prosperity."[5]

If we desire for the Word to "take root" in our lives so we produce a harvest that pleases God (Matthew 13:23), we must ponder, reflect, and meditate on what we read and study in the Bible. As we meditate, we can ask ourselves some questions:

1. What does this passage teach me about God?
2. What does this passage teach me about the church?
3. What does this passage teach me about the world?
4. What does this passage teach me about myself? About my own desires and motives?
5. Does this passage require that I take action? If so, what action should I take?
6. What do I need to confess and/or repent of?
7. What have I learned from this passage that will help me focus on God and strive for His glory?

Apply: The degree to which we study, memorize, and meditate on God's Word is the degree to which we understand how it applies to our lives. But understanding *how* the Word applies is not enough; we must actually apply it (James 1:22). Application implies action, and obedient action is the final step in allowing God's Word to come to life in our lives. The application of Scripture enforces and further enlightens our study, and it also serves to sharpen our discernment, helping us to better distinguish between good and evil (Hebrews 5:14).

As a final word, it is important to note that we are not alone in trying to understand and apply God's Word to our lives. God has filled us with His Spirit (John 14:16–17) who speaks to us, leading and guiding us into all truth (John 16:13). For this reason, Paul instructs believers to "live by the Spirit" (Galatians 5:16), for He is a very present help in our time of need (Psalm 46:1). The Spirit will faithfully guide us into the will of God, causing us to do what is right (Ezekiel 36:26–28; Philippians 2:13). Who better to teach how to live according to all that is written in the Bible than the One who inspired the Bible to begin with—the Holy Spirit Himself? Let us do our part by hiding the Word in our hearts and obeying the Holy Spirit as He draws that Word out of us.

Question: Why is Bible memorization important?

Answer: Memorizing Scripture is perhaps the single most crucial element of spiritual growth and victory over sin. The Word of God is powerful because it is "God-breathed" from the mind of the Holy Spirit (2 Timothy 3:16–17), and when we fill our minds with His words by memorizing Scripture, we avail ourselves of the most powerful spiritual tool there is.

When we memorize the Word of God, several things happen. Psalm 119:11 tells us the psalmist hid God's Word in his heart so that he would not sin against Him. Not only did the psalmist hear and read the Word, but he also internalized it and laid it up in his mind for future use. The Word of God is the believer's most potent weapon against sin, and when we memorize it, we have a strong tool for promoting godliness and righteous living. Hebrews 4:12 tells us the Word of God is "living and active," meaning that it has supernatural power to mold us into Christlikeness.

Ephesians 6:13–17 describes the believer's armor in the battle against Satan and the world. Each element of the armor is defensive—except one. The only offensive weapon is the "sword of the Spirit, which is the word of God" (verse 17). Just as Jesus used God's Word to fend off attacks of Satan (Matthew 4:1–11), so must we use the same weapon. Bible memorization ensures that we will have the appropriate truths in mind to effectively respond to the evil one who seeks to tempt us into sin (1 Peter 5:8). Romans 12:2 exhorts us to "renew" our minds so that we are no longer influenced by the thinking of the world. A vital tool in renewing our minds is Scripture memorization.

Memorizing Scripture is the privilege and responsibility of every Christian. There are several excellent Scripture memory systems available, but even without a structured method, anyone can start with key verses of the Christian faith—such as John 3:16 and Ephesians 2:8–9—and continue to build verse upon verse. The trick is to continually review the ones already memorized before adding any new ones. Whatever Bible memorization method one chooses, the benefits are victory over sin, strengthened faith, and joy in the Christian life.

Question: Why is it so hard to understand the Bible?

Answer: Everyone, to varying degrees, struggles with trying to understand certain aspects of the Bible. Even after nearly 2,000 years of church history, there are some Bible passages that leave the most brilliant of Bible scholars speculating about the correct meaning. Why does it take so much effort to fully understand the Bible? Before we attempt an answer, it should be said that God did not communicate indistinctly. Ultimately, the message of God's Word is perfectly clear.

There are several factors that can make the Bible hard to understand. First, there is a time and culture difference. The Bible was written between 3,400 and 1,900 years ago, and the culture in which the Bible was written was very different from most of today's cultures. The actions of nomadic, Middle Eastern shepherds in 1800 BC often do not make much sense to, say, computer programmers in 21st-century America. It is important that, when trying to comprehend the Bible, we identify and understand the culture in which it was written.

Second, the Bible contains different types of literature, including history, law, poetry, songs, wisdom, prophecy, personal letters, and apocalyptic literature. Historical literature must be interpreted differently from wisdom literature. Poetry cannot be understood in the same way as apocalyptic writings. A personal letter, while having meaning for us today, may have a different application today than it did for the original recipients. Recognizing that the Bible contains different genres is vital in avoiding confusion and misunderstanding.

Third, we are all sinners; we all make mistakes (Ecclesiastes 7:20; Romans 3:23; 1 John 1:8). As much as we strive not to read our preconceived biases into the Bible, it is inevitable that we all occasionally do so. Sadly, at some point everyone misinterprets a passage due to an assumption of what it can or cannot mean. When we study the Bible, we must ask God to remove our biases and help us interpret His Word apart from our presuppositions. This is often difficult to do, as admitting to presupposition requires humility and a willingness to acknowledge mistakes.

By no means are these three steps all that are needed to properly understand the Bible. Entire books have been written on biblical hermeneutics (the science of biblical interpretation). However, these steps are an excellent start to understanding the Bible.

Understanding the Bible can sometimes be a difficult task, but with God's help, it is possible. Remember, if you are a believer in Jesus Christ, God's Spirit indwells you (Romans 8:9). The God who inspired Scripture (2 Timothy 3:16) is the same God who can open your mind to the understanding of His Word. It may not be easy, as God desires us to search His Word and fully explore its treasures, but such an exploration will be rewarding.

Question: Why is understanding the Bible important?

Answer: Understanding the Bible is important because the Bible is God's Word. When we open the Bible, we read God's message to us. What could be more important than understanding what the Creator of the universe has to say?

We seek to understand the Bible for the same reason a man seeks to understand a love letter from his sweetheart. God loves us and desires to restore our relationship with Him (Matthew 23:37). God communicates His love to us in the Bible (John 3:16; 1 John 3:1; 4:10).

We seek to understand the Bible for the same reason a soldier seeks to understand a dispatch from his commander. Obeying God's commands brings honor to Him and guides us in the way of life (Psalm 119). Those commands are found in the Bible (John 14:15).

We seek to understand the Bible for the same reason a mechanic seeks to understand a repair manual. Things go wrong in this world, and the Bible not only diagnoses the problem (sin) but also points out the solution (faith in Christ). "For the wages of sin is death, but the gift of God is eternal life in Christ Jesus our Lord" (Romans 6:23).

We seek to understand the Bible for the same reason a driver seeks to understand traffic signals. The Bible gives us guidance through life, showing us the road of safety and wisdom (Psalm 119:11, 105).

We seek to understand the Bible for the same reason someone in the path of a storm seeks to understand the weather report. The Bible predicts what the end times will be like, sounding a clear warning of impending judgment (Matthew 24—25; Revelation) and how to avoid it (Romans 8:1).

We seek to understand the Bible for the same reason an avid reader seeks to understand his favorite author's books. The Bible reveals to us the person and glory of God, as expressed in His Son, Jesus Christ (John 1:1–18). The more we read and understand the Bible, the more intimately we know the Author.

As Philip was traveling to Gaza, the Holy Spirit led him to a man who was reading a portion of Isaiah. Philip approached the man, saw what he was reading, and asked this very important question: "Do you understand what you are reading?" (Acts 8:30). Philip knew that *understanding* was the starting point for faith. Without understanding the Bible, we cannot apply it, obey it, or believe it.

Question: How much influence is the Bible supposed to have on society?

Answer: In Western nations, particularly in the United States, we can see the Bible's influence on many aspects of society. Everything from our laws to our work ethic to our view of marriage has been molded by a Judeo-Christian worldview. It has always been the case that the Word of God makes a difference in cultures where it is introduced. In first-century Thessalonica, a mob dragged some Christians through the streets shouting, "These who have turned the world upside down have come here too" (Acts 17:6 NKJV). It is only right that the Bible should have an influence on society as a whole, as it has an influence on the individuals within society.

God is the Creator of the world and the humans who inhabit it (Genesis 1—2). From the very beginning, God designed the world and people to "function" a certain way. When society doesn't follow the principles that God gives us in the Bible, life simply doesn't work as well. God is the only One with the insight into how life functions to our best benefit, and He shares that wisdom with us in His Word. The Bible is described in Hebrews 4:12 as "alive and active." This means, in part, that the Bible is as applicable and relevant today as it was when it was first written.

Looking back at the early stages of the United States, it is impossible not to see the influence the Bible had. Our government structure, laws, morality, education, and family values were all founded on principles that came directly from the Bible. The Founding Fathers, presidents, and foreigners visiting a young USA identified the key to the nation's success as the biblical influence embraced by its society. When a nation honors God, it develops a respect for all of God's creation. Where there is no honor of God, a society will fail to respect His creation, and people will suffer as a result.

From the beginning, people have had a choice whether or not to follow God's way. But choices always carry consequences. The Old Testament history of Israel documents the societal laws and precepts God gave them. When Israel lived by God's laws, their society functioned well, but when they deviated from God's design, their society always went downhill. Attempts today to remove the Bible's influence from society or to marginalize a biblical worldview reveal the pride of mankind that says, "We know better than the One who created us."

None of this is to say that we should establish a theocracy like that of ancient Israel. God's purposes in that system of government were for a certain time and place. However, when the Bible is properly understood, its influence on society can only lead to less crime, less divorce, less sloth, and more charity. As John Adams, the second President of the United States, wrote, "Suppose a nation in some distant Region should take the Bible for their only law Book, and every member should regulate his conduct by the precepts there exhibited! Every member would be obliged in conscience, to temperance, frugality, and industry; to justice, kindness, and charity towards his fellow men; and to piety, love, and reverence toward Almighty God ... What a Eutopia, what a Paradise would this region be."[6] Scripture says it best: "Blessed is the nation whose God is the Lord" (Psalm 33:12).

Question: Is the Bible mind control?

Answer: Some people accuse Christians of using the Bible as a mind-control tool. The only way to build a church and retain members, they say, is to use brainwashing tactics to coerce people into lifestyle and attitudinal changes. The accusation is groundless, but those who do not know the power of the Holy Spirit need some way to explain the change in people's lives.

While it is true that cults, many of whom claim to be Christian, do practice forms of mind control, true Christianity is not coercive in any way. Pastors who love the Lord desire to nourish, edify, and protect their congregations (John 21:15–18). Church leaders are to serve unselfishly and humbly, with no thought of personal gain (1 Peter 5:2–3). So, no, the Bible is not mind control, and it does not advocate mind control in the sense of brainwashing or psychological programming.

However, the Bible does speak of controlling one's mind. Repentance involves a change of mind. Christians are "made new in the attitude of [their] minds" (Ephesians 4:23). They are to be likeminded, so as to avoid quarrels (Philippians 2:2). They have been given the mind of Christ (1 Corinthians 2:16). The result is a new attitude and new behavior—a whole new creation, in fact (2 Corinthians 5:17). The change is not due to a guru's devious plan or a carefully controlled environment; the change is internal, spiritual, and real. It is due to the work of the Holy Spirit, not a human agent (Titus 3:5).

Man has a sin nature inherited from Adam (Romans 5:12). That sin nature has control of a person and causes various sins to manifest in one's life (Galatians 5:17–21). Controlled by that sin nature, man can in no way know God and please God. In fact, he is an enemy of God (Romans 5:10; 8:5–7). The Bible says that the sinner, controlled by his sinful nature, needs a new nature and deliverance from the power of sin. The person who accepts Jesus Christ as personal Savior receives that new nature (2 Peter 1:4) and is indwelt by the Holy Spirit, who gives the believer the power to say "no" to sin and "yes" to God's righteousness (Galatians 5:16; Romans 6:12–23). The believer in Christ has been set free (John 8:32). He is not obligated to obey the dictates of the sin nature anymore, for he has the freedom in Christ to do what God wants and to glorify Him in life.

The Bible is not mind control. Rather, the Bible provides an alternative to a life controlled by sin. The Bible shows us how to be Spirit-controlled. Yes, a believer will have a change of mind, as he rejects the lies he once believed and embraces the truth in Christ. The Spirit-filled believer will have a new life—a life free to serve God with enthusiasm, eternal fulfillment, and hope.

Chapter 9

QUESTIONS ABOUT EXTRA-BIBLICAL TEXTS

Contents

Question: What are the Apocryphal/Deuterocanonical books?

Answer: Roman Catholic Bibles have several more books in the Old Testament than Protestant Bibles. These books are referred to as the Apocrypha or Deuterocanonical books. The word apocrypha means "hidden," while the word deuterocanonical means "second canon." The Apocrypha/Deuterocanonicals were written in the time between the Old and New Testaments. The books of the Apocrypha are Tobit, Judith, Wisdom of Solomon, Ecclesiasticus, Baruch, the Letter of Jeremiah, Prayer of Manasseh, 1 Maccabees, and 2 Maccabees, as well as additions to the canonical books of Esther and Daniel.

The nation of Israel treated the Apocrypha/Deuterocanonical books with respect, but never accepted them as true books of the Hebrew Bible. The early Christian church debated the status of the Apocrypha/Deuterocanonicals, but few early Christians believed they belonged in the canon of Scripture. The New Testament quotes from the Old Testament hundreds of times, but nowhere quotes or alludes to any of the Apocryphal/Deuterocanonical books. In addition, the Apocrypha/Deuterocanonical books teach many things that are not true and are historically inaccurate.

While many Catholics accepted the Apocrypha/Deuterocanonicals previously, the Roman Catholic Church officially added the Apocrypha/Deuterocanonicals to their Bible at the Council of Trent in the mid-1500s, primarily in response to the Protestant Reformation. The Apocrypha/Deuterocanonicals support some of the Roman Catholic Church's beliefs and practices that are not in agreement with the Bible. Examples are praying for the dead, petitioning "saints" in heaven, worshipping angels, and "alms-giving" for atonement of sins.

Some of what the Apocrypha/Deuterocanonicals say is true and correct. However, due to the historical and theological errors, the books must be viewed as fallible historical and religious documents, not as the inspired, authoritative Word of God.

Question: What are the lost books of the Bible?

Answer: There are no "lost books" of the Bible or books that were taken out of the Bible. There are many legends and rumors of lost books, but there is no truth whatsoever to these stories. Every book that God intended and inspired to be in the Bible is in the Bible. There are literally hundreds of religious books that were written in the same time period as the books of the Bible. Some of these books contain true accounts of things that actually occurred (1 Maccabees, for example). Some contain good spiritual teaching (the Wisdom of Solomon, for example). However, these books are not inspired by God. If we read any of these books, such as the Apocrypha, we have to treat them as fallible historical books and not as the inspired, inerrant Word of God (2 Timothy 3:16–17).

Take, for example, the Gospel of Thomas. This book was a forgery written in the third or fourth century AD, claiming to have been written by the apostle Thomas when in fact it was not. The early church fathers almost universally rejected the Gospel of Thomas as heretical. It contains many false accounts of things that Jesus supposedly said and did. None of it (or at best very little of it) is true. The Epistle of Barnabas was not written by the biblical Barnabas, but by an imposter. The same can be said of the Gospel of Philip, the Apocalypse of Peter, etc.

There is one God. The Bible has one Creator. It is one book. It has one plan of grace, recorded from initiation through execution to consummation. From predestination to glorification, the Bible is the story of God redeeming His chosen people for the praise of His glory. As God's redemptive purposes and plan unfold in Scripture, the recurring themes are the character of God, the judgment for sin and disobedience, the blessing for faith and obedience, the Savior and His sacrifice for sin, and the coming kingdom and glory. It is God's intention that we know and understand these five themes. Our eternal destinies depend on faith in the Christ of the Bible. It is unthinkable that God would allow some vital information to be "lost" in any way. The Bible is complete, in order that we who read and understand it might also be "thoroughly equipped for every good work" (2 Timothy 3:16–17).

Question: What is the book of Enoch, and should it be in the Bible?

Answer: The Book of Enoch is any of several pseudepigraphal works (falsely attributed works; texts whose claimed authorship is unfounded) that attribute themselves to Enoch. Enoch lived before the Flood; he was the son of Jared (Genesis 5:18) and great-grandfather of Noah. Enoch is also one of the three people in the Bible taken up to heaven while still alive (the only others being Elijah and Jesus). As the Bible says, "Enoch walked with God; then he was no more, because God took him away" (Genesis 5:24; see also Hebrews 11:5). Most commonly, the phrase "Book of Enoch" refers to 1 Enoch, which exists only in the Ethiopic language.

The biblical book of Jude quotes from the Book of Enoch in verses 14–15, "Enoch, the seventh from Adam, prophesied about these men: 'See, the Lord is coming with thousands upon thousands of his holy ones to judge everyone, and to convict all the ungodly of all the ungodly acts they have done in the ungodly way, and of all the harsh words ungodly sinners have spoken against him.'" But this does not mean the Book of Enoch is inspired by God and should be in the Bible.

Jude's quote is not the only quote in the Bible from a non-biblical source. The apostle Paul quotes Epimenides in Titus 1:12, but that does not mean we should give any additional authority to Epimenides' writings. The same is true with Jude, verses 14–15. Jude's quoting from the Book of Enoch does not indicate the entire Book of Enoch is inspired, or even true. All it means is that particular verse is true.

It is interesting to note that no scholars believe the Book of Enoch was truly written by the Enoch of the Bible. Evidently, though, the words quoted by Jude were genuinely something Enoch prophesied, or the Bible would not attribute them to him. "Enoch, the seventh from Adam, prophesied about these men …" (Jude 14). This saying of Enoch's was evidently handed down by tradition and eventually recorded in the Book of Enoch.

We should treat the Book of Enoch (and the other books like it) in the same manner we do the other pseudepigraphal writings.

Some of what the Pseudepigrapha says may be true, but much of it is false and historically inaccurate. The only reason we know that a small portion of 1 Enoch is true is that it is quoted by Jude.

Question: What are the Gnostic gospels?

Answer: The Gnostic gospels are writings by early "Christian" Gnostics. After the first century of Christianity, two primary divisions developed—orthodox and Gnostic. The orthodox Christians held to the books we now have in the Bible and to what is today considered orthodox theology. The Gnostic Christians, if they can truly be described as Christians, held a distinctly different view of the Bible, of Jesus Christ, of salvation, and of virtually every other major Christian doctrine. However, they did not have any apostolic writings to give legitimacy to their beliefs.

That is why and how the Gnostic gospels were created. The Gnostics fraudulently attached the names of famous Christians to their writings, such as the Gospel of Thomas, the Gospel of Philip, the Gospel of Mary, etc. The discovery of the Nag Hammadi library in northern Egypt in 1945 represented a major discovery of Gnostic gospels. These Gnostic gospels are often pointed to as supposed "lost books of the Bible."

So, what are we to make of the Gnostic gospels? Should some or all of them be in the Bible? No, they should not. First, as pointed out above, the Gnostic gospels are forgeries, fraudulently written in the names of the apostles in order to give them legitimacy in the early church. Thankfully, the early church fathers were nearly unanimous in recognizing the Gnostic gospels as promoting false teachings. There are countless contradictions between the Gnostic gospels and the true gospels of Matthew, Mark, Luke, and John. The Gnostic gospels can be a good resource for the study of early Christian heresies, but they should be rejected as sources of truth. They do not belong in the Bible and do not represent the genuine Christian faith.

Question: What is the Q gospel? Is there any evidence for the gospel of Q?

Answer: The "gospel of Q" gets its title from the German word *quelle*, which means "source." The whole idea of a Q gospel is based on the concept that the Synoptic Gospels (Matthew, Mark, and Luke) are so similar that they must have copied from each other and/or another source. This other source has been given the name "Q." The predominant arguments for the existence of a Q gospel are essentially these:

1. The gospels of Matthew, Mark, and Luke were written after AD 70 and therefore could not have been written by the apostle Matthew, John Mark, or Luke the doctor.
2. Since the authors of the Gospels were not firsthand witnesses, they must have used other sources.
3. Since Mark is the shortest gospel and has the least original material, Mark was written first and Matthew and Luke used Mark as a source.
4. Since there are many similarities in Matthew and Luke that do not occur in Mark, Matthew and Luke must have had another source in addition to Mark. This source, "Q," was likely a collection of sayings of Jesus, similar to the Gospel of Thomas.

When considering the possibility of a Q gospel, it is important to remember that no evidence whatsoever has been found for the existence of a Q gospel—not even a single manuscript fragment of "Q" has been unearthed. None of the early church fathers mentioned anything that could have been the Q gospel. There is also strong evidence that the gospels of Matthew, Mark, and Luke were written between AD 50 and 65, not after AD 70. Many of the early church fathers attributed the Gospels to the apostle Matthew, John Mark, and Luke the doctor, and they were nearly unanimous that Matthew was written first. If Matthew, Mark, and Luke wrote the Gospels, then we have a record written by actual eyewitnesses and/or close companions of eyewitnesses of what Jesus did and said. Accounts of the same events will naturally include many similarities.

Finally, there is nothing wrong with the idea of the gospel writers' using the other gospels as sources. Luke states in Luke chapter 1 that he used sources. It is possible that Matthew and Luke used Mark as a source. It is even possible that there was another source in addition to Mark. The use of a document containing the sayings of Jesus does not take away from the inspiration of Scripture. However, the whole reason for the Q gospel hypothesis—and the reason it should be rejected—is the presupposition that the Synoptic Gospels are not divinely inspired.

The vast majority of those who promote the Q gospel concept do not believe the Gospels were written by the apostles and their close associates or that the Gospels were written within the generation of the apostles. They do not believe it possible that two or three authors could use the same words without copying from each other. Crucially, most "Q" advocates reject the Holy Spirit's inspiring the gospel writers to accurately record the words and works of Jesus Christ. Again, the use of a "Q" source is not the problem. The problem is the reason why most Q gospel advocates believe a "Q" was used—namely, a denial of the inspiration of Scripture (Matthew 5:18; 24:35; John 10:35; 17:17; 1 Corinthians 2:13; 2 Timothy 3:16–17; 2 Peter 1:20–21).

Chapter 10

QUESTIONS ABOUT
BIBLICAL CRITICISM

Contents

169

Question: What is textual criticism?

Answer: Simply stated, textual criticism is a method used to determine what the original manuscripts of the Bible said. The original manuscripts of the Bible are either lost, hidden, or no longer in existence. What we do have is tens of thousands of copies of the original manuscripts dating from the first to 15th centuries AD for the New Testament and from the fourth century BC to the 15th century AD for the Old Testament. In these manuscripts, there are many minor and a few somewhat major differences. Textual criticism is the study of these manuscripts in an attempt to determine what the original reading actually was.

There are three primary methods of textual criticism. The first is to use the *Textus Receptus* ("Received Text"). The *Textus Receptus* is a Greek-language manuscript of the New Testament compiled by a scholar named Erasmus in the 1500s AD, using all the manuscripts to which he had access. The *Textus Receptus* is the textual basis for the King James Version and the New King James Version.

A second method is to use what is known as the Majority Text. The Majority Text takes all of the manuscripts available today, compares them, and chooses a reading based on which one occurs the most. For example, if 748 manuscripts read "he said," and 1,429 manuscripts read "they said," the Majority Text will go with "they said" as the most likely original reading. There are no major Bible translations based on the Majority Text.

The third method is known as the critical or eclectic method. The eclectic method considers a large number of manuscripts and weights them according to age, location, and other criteria. Both external and internal evidences are examined. In looking at external evidence, we ask these questions: In how many manuscripts does the reading occur? What are the dates for these manuscripts? In what region of the world were these manuscripts found? Internal evidence prompts these questions: What could have caused these varying readings? Which reading can possibly explain the origin of the other readings? The New International

Version, New American Standard Bible, New Living Translation, and most other Bible translations use the Eclectic or Critical Text.

Which method results in the most accurate wording of the Bible? That is where the debate begins. At first blush, the Majority Text, with its "majority rules" and "democratic" approach, seems to be the way to go. However, there is a reason the Majority Text is rarely used. In the first few centuries of the church, the vast majority of Christians spoke and wrote in Greek. Starting in the fourth century AD, Latin overtook Greek as the most common language, especially in the church. Copies of the New Testament began to be made in Latin.

However, in the East, Greek continued as the dominant language of the church for over 1,000 more years. As a result, the vast majority of Greek manuscripts are from the Eastern/Byzantine region. These Byzantine manuscripts are all very similar to each other, likely originating with the same few Greek manuscripts, but they have numerous differences with the manuscripts found in the West. So, it essentially boils down to this: the Eastern reading has an "unfair advantage" in the Majority Text, due to the sheer number of Byzantine copies. To illustrate, let's say we start with three manuscripts. One is copied 100 times, another 200 times, and the third 5,000 times. The group of copies based on the third manuscript is going to have "majority rule." However, the third group is no more likely to have the original reading than the first or second group. It only has *more copies*, and quantity of copies does not guarantee accuracy of content.

How does the critical/eclectic method work? If you compare John 5:1–9 in the King James Version (based on the *Textus Receptus*) and the New International Version (based on the Critical Text), you will notice that verse 4 is missing from the NIV. In the KJV, John 5:4 reads, "For an angel went down at a certain season into the pool, and troubled the water: whosoever then first after the troubling of the water stepped in was made whole of whatsoever disease he had." Why is this verse missing from the NIV (and the other Bible translations that use the Critical Text)? Here are the factors that led to the "omission" of John 5:4 in the Critical Text:

1) John 5:4 does not occur in most of the oldest manuscripts. 2) John 5:4 occurs in all of the Byzantine manuscripts but not in many of the non-Eastern manuscripts. 3) It is more likely that a scribe would *add* an explanation than *remove* an explanation. John 5:4 explains why the crippled man wanted to get into the pool. Why would a scribe *remove* this verse? That would not make sense. It *would* make sense if a scribe, trying to be helpful, added a brief explanation of a local tradition to clarify the reason for the crippled man's presence at the pool. Most likely, the scribe added his explanation in the *margin* of the copy he was making, and a later scribe, making his own copy, inserted the marginal note, mistaking it for an actual verse. Taking all of this into account, the Critical/Eclectic Text does not include John 5:4.

No matter what method of textual criticism you believe is correct, this is an issue that should be discussed with grace, respect, and kindness. Christians can and do disagree on this issue. We can debate the methods, but we should not attack the motivations and character of those with whom we disagree. Those devoted to Christ all have the same goal in textual criticism—to determine what is most likely to be the original wording of the Bible. Some simply have different methods to achieve that goal.

Question: What are redaction criticism and higher criticism?

Answer: Redaction criticism and higher criticism are just a few of many forms of biblical criticism. The intent of biblical criticism is purportedly to investigate the Scriptures and determine each book's authorship, historicity, date of writing, etc., in order to more fully understand the biblical text. Sadly, most methods of biblical criticism are used in attempts to destroy the authority of the Bible.

Biblical criticism takes two major forms: higher and lower criticism. Lower criticism, or textual criticism, focuses on the actual text of Scripture. Its goal is to determine, as far as possible, the original wording of the authors of the Bible, based on extant manuscripts. Higher criticism, which grew out of rationalism and naturalism, takes a secular approach and focuses on the human origin of the text. Its goal is to determine who the "real" authors were and what influenced them to write what they did. Higher criticism often presupposes the non-historicity of the biblical narrative and the authors' dependence on outside sources in their writing.

Redaction criticism is a form of higher criticism. Redaction critics focus on the process that led to the Bible in its final form as literature. The assumption is that various portions of Scripture were compiled through the centuries from oral tradition and other sources and that someone finally edited the compilation, "redacting" or revising the text to serve a personal theological or literary purpose. Redaction criticism tries to identify supposed "changes" made to the Bible—how "legends" were amplified, which narratives were combined, and *why*. There is no thought given to the inspiration of the Bible; redaction criticism approaches the Bible as a purely human work.

Originally, redaction criticism was limited to the Synoptic Gospels. Critics, working under the assumption that Matthew, Mark, and Luke didn't really write those books and that Jesus didn't really perform miracles, attempted to figure out how, when, and why the "mythical" portions of the Gospels came to be. They also assumed that Jesus never said most of what was attributed to Him, so they came up with theories on who put words in Jesus' mouth and what their motivation could have been. Redaction criticism has been applied to other portions of Scripture, as well. Thus, there are critics who deny Mosaic authorship of the Pentateuch and promote the idea that the Old Testament is simply a compilation of oral traditions that were not actually written down until after Israel was taken into captivity to Babylon in 586 BC.

Of course, if Moses did not actually write the Pentateuch, then Exodus 24:4 and all the other passages that attribute the writing to Moses are falsehoods. If the gospel of John was not written by John, then the author (who claimed to be John the disciple in John 21:24) is a liar, and the gospel is a forgery. The whole Bible becomes suspect. But that's the point of redaction criticism and other forms of higher criticism—to cast aspersions on the biblical text, to ask, with the serpent in the garden, "Did God really say?" (Genesis 3:1).

Higher criticism is an attempt by some liberal theologians to deny the Holy Spirit's work in the production of an accurate, reliable written Word of God. But the Holy Spirit *was* involved: "All scripture is inspired by God" (2 Timothy 3:16 NASB). God gave men the words He wanted recorded. The apostle Peter wrote, "Above all, you must understand that no prophecy of Scripture came about by the prophet's own interpretation. For prophecy never had its origin in the will of man" (2 Peter 1:20–21). The content of Scripture was not dreamed up in the mind of man, created by people just wanting to write something down. Peter continues, "But men moved by the Holy Spirit spoke from God" (2 Peter 1:21). The Holy Spirit told them what He wanted them to write. God was behind the scenes directing and guiding the writing. As much as some people hate to admit it, revelation trumps reason.

Question: What is the documentary hypothesis?

Answer: The documentary hypothesis is essentially an attempt to take the supernatural out of the Pentateuch and to deny its Mosaic authorship. The accounts of the Red Sea crossing, the manna in the wilderness, the provision of water from a solid rock, etc., are considered stories from oral tradition, thus making the miraculous happenings mere products of imaginative storytellers and not events that actually happened and were recorded by eyewitnesses. The documentary hypothesis, along with the JEDP theory (described later in this book), denies that Moses wrote the Pentateuch and instead ascribes its authorship to four (or more) different authors/redactors spread out over several hundreds of years. The documentary hypothesis is liberal theology's attempt to call the veracity of the Pentateuch into question.

Proponents of the documentary hypothesis believe as follows: instead of placing the writing of the Pentateuch around 1400 BC (when Moses died), the timeframe has shifted 1,000 years to around 400 BC. A 1,000-year-old memory, even when passed down as faithfully as possible, will change the story of the original events. Remember, the Pentateuch was still being written during the time when the Israelites wandered in the wilderness as a result of their rebellion against God. To finally record this journey some 1,000 years after it happened is to invite speculation on the genuineness of the original journey. Liberal theologians have, through the years, tried to weaken the Word of God, and one way they do that is by casting doubt on the historicity and authorship of the Pentateuch.

The question is whether this liberal theological view has any basis in reality. The date for the writing of the Pentateuch is a case in point. Liberal theology dates the writing of the Pentateuch from 400 BC, which is after the Babylonian Captivity. This means that Moses could not possibly have written the Pentateuch, for he died about 1,000 years before that. However, Jesus said in Mark 12:26, "Have you not read in the book of Moses, in the account of the bush, how God said to him, 'I am the God of Abraham, the God of Isaac, and the God of Jacob'?" Jesus states plainly that Moses wrote the account of the burning bush in Exodus 3. To date the Pentateuch some 1,000 years after the death of Moses is to deny Jesus' words, for He specifies that Exodus is part of "the book of Moses."

There is strong evidence that Moses also wrote the other books of the Pentateuch, disproving the whole documentary hypothesis. Peter, in Acts 3:22, comments on Deuteronomy 18:15 and credits Moses as being the author of that passage. Paul, in Romans 10:5, says, "Moses writes this," and then proceeds to quote Leviticus 18:5.

The documentary hypothesis calls into question the testimonies of Jesus, Peter, and Paul, for all of them testified that Moses wrote at least three of the books of the Pentateuch. Jewish history and tradition also credit Moses as the author of the Pentateuch, giving no support whatsoever to the documentary hypothesis. The documentary hypothesis is only a hypothesis; it has never been proved, no matter how many liberal theologians claim that it has been.

Question: What is the JEDP Theory?

Answer: In brief, the JEDP theory states that the first five books of the Bible—Genesis, Exodus, Leviticus, Numbers, and Deuteronomy—were not written entirely by Moses, who died in the 1400s BC, but also by different authors/compilers after Moses. The theory is based on the fact that different names for God are used in different portions of the Pentateuch, and there are detectable differences in linguistic style. The letters of the JEDP theory stand for the four supposed authors: the author who uses *Jehovah* for God's name, the author who uses *Elohim* for God's name, the author of **Deuteronomy**, and the Priestly author of Leviticus. The JEDP theory goes on to state that the different portions of the Pentateuch were likely compiled in the fourth century BC, possibly by Ezra.

So, why are there different names for God in books supposedly written by a single author? For example, Genesis chapter 1 uses the name *Elohim* while Genesis chapter 2 uses the name *YHWH*. Patterns like this occur quite frequently in the Pentateuch. The answer is simple. Moses used God's names to make a point. In Genesis chapter 1, God is *Elohim*, the mighty Creator God. In Genesis chapter 2, God is *YHWH*, the personal God who created and relates to humanity. This does not point to different authors but to a single author using God's various names to emphasize a point and describe different aspects of God's character.

Regarding the different writing styles, should we not expect an author to have a different style when he is writing history (Genesis), writing legal statutes (Exodus, Deuteronomy), and writing intricate details of the sacrificial system (Leviticus)? The JEDP theory takes the explainable differences in the Pentateuch and invents an elaborate theory that has no basis in reality or history. No J, E, D, or P document has ever been discovered. No ancient Jewish or Christian scholar has even hinted that such documents existed.

The most powerful argument against the JEDP theory is the Bible itself. Jesus, in Mark 12:26, said, "Now about the dead rising—have you not read in the book of Moses, in the account of the bush, how God said to him, 'I am the God of Abraham, the God of Isaac, and the God of Jacob'?" Jesus says plainly that Moses wrote the account of the burning bush in Exodus 3. Peter, in Acts 3:22, comments on a passage in Deuteronomy 18:15 and credits Moses as being the author of that passage. Paul, in Romans 10:5, talks about the righteousness Moses describes in Leviticus 18:5, testifying that Moses is the author of Leviticus. So, we have Jesus showing that Moses was the author of Exodus, Peter (in Acts) showing that Moses wrote Deuteronomy, and Paul saying that Moses was the author of Leviticus. In order for the JEDP theory to be true, Jesus, Peter, and Paul must all either be liars or be in error in their understanding of the Old Testament. Let us put our faith in Jesus and the human authors of Scripture rather than the ridiculous and baseless JEDP theory (2 Timothy 3:16–17).

Question: What is the Synoptic Problem?

Answer: When the first three gospels are compared—Matthew, Mark, and Luke—it is unmistakable that the accounts are very similar to one another in content and expression. As a result, Matthew, Mark, and Luke are referred to as the "Synoptic Gospels." The word *synoptic* basically means "to see together with a common view." The many similarities between the Synoptic Gospels have led some to wonder if the gospel authors shared material or had a common source, another written account of Christ's birth, life, ministry, death, and resurrection from which they obtained the material for their gospels. The question of how to explain the similarities and differences among the Synoptic Gospels is called the Synoptic Problem.

Some argue that Matthew, Mark, and Luke are so similar that they must have used each other's gospels or another common source. This supposed "source" has been given the title "Q" from the German word *quelle*, which means "source." Is there any evidence for a "Q" document? No, there is not. No portion or fragment of a "Q" document has ever been discovered. None of the early church fathers ever mentioned a gospel "source" in their writings. "Q" is the invention of liberal scholars who deny the inspiration of the Bible. They believe the Bible to be nothing more than a work of literature, subject to the same criticism given to other works of literature. Again, there is no evidence whatsoever for a "Q" document—biblically, theologically, or historically.

If Matthew, Mark, and Luke did not use a "Q" document, why are their gospels so similar? There are several possible explanations. It is possible that, whichever gospel was written first (likely Mark, although the church fathers reported that Matthew was written first), the other gospel writers had access to it. There is absolutely no problem with the idea that Matthew and/or Luke copied some text from Mark's gospel and used it in their gospels. Perhaps Luke had access to Mark and Matthew and used texts from both of them in his own gospel. Luke 1:1–4 tells us, "Many have undertaken to draw up an account of the things that have been fulfilled among us, just as they were handed down to us by those who from the first were eyewitnesses and servants of the word. Therefore, since I myself have carefully investigated everything from the beginning, it seemed good also to me to write an orderly account for you, most excellent Theophilus, so that you may know the certainty of the things you have been taught."

Ultimately, the Synoptic "Problem" is not as big a problem as some try to make it out to be. The explanation as to why the Synoptic Gospels are so similar is that they are all inspired by the same Holy Spirit and are all written by people who witnessed or were told about the same events. The gospel of Matthew was written by Matthew the apostle, one of the twelve who followed Jesus and were commissioned by Him. The gospel of Mark was written by John Mark, a close associate of the apostle Peter, another one of the twelve. The gospel of Luke was written by Luke, a close associate of the apostle Paul. Why would we not expect their accounts to be very similar to one another? Each of the gospels is ultimately inspired by the Holy Spirit (2 Timothy 3:16–17; 2 Peter 1:20–21). Therefore, we should expect coherence and unity.

Chapter 11

MISCELLANEOUS QUESTIONS ABOUT THE BIBLE

Contents

What is the biblical significance of the number seven?

Does the warning in Revelation 22:18–19 apply to the entire Bible or just to the book of Revelation?

What are the modern equivalents of biblical weights and measures?

What is bibliolatry?

Question: Can/Should we interpret the Bible as literal?

Answer: Not only *can* we take the Bible literally, but we *must* take the Bible literally. A literal approach to interpretation is the only way to determine what God is trying to communicate to us. When we read any piece of literature, we must determine what the author meant to communicate. Many will read a verse or passage of Scripture and then create their own definitions for the words, phrases, or paragraphs, ignoring the context and author's intent. But this is not what God intended, which is why God tells us to correctly handle the Word of truth (2 Timothy 2:15).

One reason we should take the Bible literally is that the Lord Jesus Christ took it literally. Whenever the Lord Jesus quoted from the Old Testament, it was always clear that He believed in its literal interpretation. For example, when Satan tempted Jesus in Luke 4, Jesus responded by quoting the Old Testament. If God's commands in Deuteronomy 8:3, 6:13, and 6:16 were not literal, Jesus would not have used them, and they would have been powerless to stop Satan's mouth, which is what they did.

The disciples also took the commands of Christ (which are part of the Bible) literally. Jesus commanded the disciples to go and make more disciples in Matthew 28:19–20. In the book of Acts, we find that the disciples took Jesus' command literally as they went throughout the known world preaching the gospel and telling everyone to "believe in the Lord Jesus, and you will be saved" (Acts 16:31). We, too, must take Jesus' words literally. How can we be sure of our salvation if we do not believe that He came to seek and save the lost (Luke 19:10), pay the penalty for our sin (Matthew 26:28), and provide eternal life (John 6:54)?

Taking the Bible literally still allows for figures of speech. An example of a figure of speech is someone saying, "The sun is rising." Technically, the sun does not rise; the earth rotates in a way that makes it seem that the sun is rising. Yet almost everyone understands figures of speech well enough to allow for this type of communication. There are obvious figures of speech in the Bible that are not to be taken literally. (See Psalm 17:8, for example.)

Finally, when we make ourselves the final arbiters of which parts of the Bible are literal and which are not, we elevate ourselves above God. He gave us His Word to communicate with us. The confusion and distortions that would inevitably result from a non-literal interpretation would essentially render the Scriptures null and void. The Bible is God's Word to us, and He meant it to be believed—literally and completely.

Question: Are the miracles in the Bible to be taken literally?

Answer: Yes, the miracles of the Bible are to be taken literally. All Scripture is to be taken literally, except those portions that are clearly intended to be symbolic. An example of symbolism is Psalm 17:8. We are not *literally* apples in God's eye, nor does God *literally* have wings. But the miracles described in the Bible are not symbolic happenings; they are real events that actually happened. Each of the miracles in the Bible served a purpose and accomplished something to further God's plan.

The earliest and most profound miracle of all was that of creation. God created everything *ex nihilo*—from nothing—and each succeeding miracle reinforced His incredible power. The book of Exodus is filled with miraculous events God used to bring about His will. The plagues on Egypt, beginning with the Nile being turned to blood (Exodus 7:17) and ending with the death of the firstborn of Egypt (Exodus 12:12), were literal events that eventually caused Pharaoh to free the Israelites from bondage. If the plagues never happened, why did Pharaoh let the people go? And if the death of the firstborn was not literal, then there was no reason for the Israelites to apply blood to their doorposts. If that were the case, then the foreshadowing of Jesus' shed blood on the cross is voided, which, in turn, puts the crucifixion itself into doubt. Once we begin to doubt the reality of any biblical miracle, we must discount everything the Bible says resulted from that miracle, which ultimately casts doubt on all of Scripture.

Among the best-known Old Testament miracles are the parting of the Red Sea (Exodus 14) and the subsequent drowning of Pharaoh and his army. If this part of the narrative is symbolic, then can we trust the rest of the story? Did the Israelites really leave Egypt? Did Pharaoh's army really follow them, and, if so, how did the Israelites escape? Psalm 78 is one of many passages where God reminds the Israelites of the miracles He performed in releasing them from Egyptian bondage. These miracles surrounding the exodus also had the purpose of increasing awareness of God Jehovah among the surrounding nations and proving that He is the one, true God (Joshua 2:10). The other nations' idols of wood and stone were incapable of such miracles.

In the New Testament, Jesus performed numerous miracles, beginning with the one at the wedding in Cana where He turned water into wine (John 2:1–10). His most spectacular miracle was probably the raising of Lazarus after Lazarus had been dead four days (John 11). All the miracles Jesus did were to prove that He was indeed who He said He was—the Son of God. When He calmed the storm in Matthew 8, even the disciples were astonished: "The men were amazed and asked, 'What kind of man is this? Even the winds and the waves obey him!'" (verse 27). If Jesus' miracles were not real, then the Gospel accounts of Jesus' healings are just nice stories, and those people remained afflicted by diseases, calling into doubt His compassion (Matthew 14:14; Mark 1:41). If He didn't really feed thousands of people with a few loaves and fishes (John 6), those people remained hungry, and Jesus' words "You are looking for me … because you ate the loaves and had your fill" (verse 26) have no meaning at all. But Jesus did heal, He did create food for thousands, He did turn water into wine, and He did raise Lazarus from the dead. John 2:23 tells us that many believed in Him because of the miracles.

All the miracles recorded in the Bible had a purpose—to prove that God is like no one else, that He has complete control of creation, and that, if He can do all these miraculous things, nothing in our lives is too hard for Him to handle. He wants us to trust Him. If the miracles in the Bible did not occur, then how can we trust anything else the Bible tells us? How can we trust the Bible's good news of eternal life through Christ? When we begin to call any part of Scripture into doubt, all of God's Word becomes suspect, and we open the door for the lies and distortions of Satan as he seeks to destroy our faith (1 Peter 5:8). The Bible is to be read and understood literally, including the accounts of miracles.

Question: How did people know about God before the Bible?

Answer: Even before people had the written Word of God, they had the ability to receive, understand, and obey God. In fact, there are many areas of the world today where Bibles are not available, yet people can and do know about God. The issue is one of revelation—God's revealing to man what He wants us to know about Himself. While there has not always been a Bible, there have always been means for man to receive and understand God's revelation. There are two categories of revelation: general and special.

General revelation is what God communicates universally to all mankind. The external aspect of general revelation is creation and the fact that God must be the cause or source of it. Because the universe exists, and because there must be a cause for its existence, God must also exist. Romans 1:20 says, "For since the creation of the world God's invisible qualities—his eternal power and divine nature—have been clearly seen, being understood from what has been made, so that men are without excuse." All men and women everywhere can look at creation and know that God exists. Psalm 19:1–4 further explains that creation speaks clearly of God in a language that all understand. "There is no speech or language where their voice is not heard" (verse 3). The revelation from nature is clear. No one can excuse himself because of ignorance. There is no alibi for the atheist, and there is no excuse for the agnostic.

Another aspect of general revelation—that which God has revealed to everyone—is the conscience. This is internal. "What may be known of God is manifest in them" (Romans 1:19 KJV).

People, because they possess an immaterial, spiritual nature, are conscious that God exists. These two aspects of general revelation are illustrated in many stories of missionaries meeting native tribes who have never seen a Bible or heard of Jesus. Yet, when the plan of salvation is presented to them, they know that God exists because they see evidence of Him in nature, and they know they need a Savior because their consciences convict them of their sin and their need of Him.

In addition to general revelation, there is special revelation that God uses to teach mankind about Himself and His will. Special revelation does not come to all people, but only to certain people at certain times. Examples from Scripture of special revelation are the lot (Acts 1:21–26; also Proverbs 16:33), the Urim and Thummim (a special type of lot used by the High Priest—see Exodus 28:30; Numbers 27:21; Deuteronomy 33:8; 1 Samuel 28:6; and Ezra 2:63), dreams and visions (Genesis 20:3, 6; 31:11–13, 24; Joel 2:28), appearances of the Angel of the Lord (Genesis 16:7–14; Exodus 3:2; 2 Samuel 24:16; Zechariah 1:12), and the ministry of the prophets (2 Samuel 23:2; Zechariah 1:1). These references are not an exhaustive list of every occurrence, but they should serve as good examples of special revelation.

The Bible is also a form of special revelation. It is in a category all by itself, however, because it renders other forms of special revelation unnecessary for today. The Bible is the written form of all the information God wants us to know about Him and His plan. In fact, the Bible contains everything we need to know in order to have a relationship with God.

Of course, the clearest revelation of God was His Son, Jesus Christ (John 1:14; Hebrews 1:3), called the Word of God in John 1:1. When Jesus took on human form to walk this earth among us, that act alone spoke volumes. When He died for our sins on the cross, we were left with no doubt that God is love (1 John 4:10).

Before the Bible as we know it was available, God used many means to reveal Himself and His will to mankind. It is amazing to think that God did not use just one form, but many. It makes us thankful that God gave us His written Word and preserved it for us today. We are not at the mercy of someone else telling us what God has said; we can study what He said for ourselves!

Question: Why is there so much confusion regarding the teachings of the Bible?

Answer: God gave us the Bible to teach us about Him and His ways, and since God is not a God of confusion (1 Corinthians 14:33), any and all confusion must come from the destructive forces of the world, the flesh, and the devil. The "world" refers to an ungodly world system and its people who do not understand or care about the Word of God; the "flesh" is the lingering sinful nature Christians possess that corrupts their godly walk; and the "devil" refers to Satan and his demons who twist God's Word, often while masquerading as angels of light (2 Corinthians 11:14–15).

While Satan uses various methods to blind mankind to the truth of the Word, most confusion results from our own laziness and/or heeding of false teaching. Ultimately, and most tragically, confusion about the Bible can lead to a false hope of salvation. And that is Satan's goal. When Satan tempted Jesus, he used misinterpretations of the Word of God for his attacks. Satan does the same thing today, taking a truth of Scripture and misapplying it. Satan is skilled at twisting the Word of God just enough so that it produces disastrous consequences, while still sounding like the Word of God.

Sometimes confusion over what the Bible teaches originates with poor Bible translations, or even intentionally distorted translations. More often, though, confusion results from a lack of serious study among believers and the false preachers, teachers, and writers (2 Corinthians 11:12–13) who are found on radio, television, and the Internet. These false prophets take even proper translations and, through both ignorance and design, twist and distort the Word of God to promote their own agenda or appeal to the thinking of the world. Instead of lazy Bible study and relying solely on others to teach us the Word of God, we should study God's Word diligently ourselves and rely on the Holy Spirit. He will open our hearts to God's truth concerning Himself and His salvation.

Most deadly is the rampant confusion regarding the truth of the gospel. While Scripture teaches that Jesus Christ is the only way, the only truth, and the only life (John 14:6; Acts 4:12), today many (even some who call themselves evangelical Christians) believe that heaven can be gained by other ways and other religions. But, in spite of the confusion, the sheep will still hear the voice of the Shepherd and will follow only Him (John 10:27). Those who do not belong to the Shepherd "will not put up with sound doctrine. Instead, to suit their own desires, they will gather around them a great number of teachers to say what their itching ears want to hear" (2 Timothy 4:3). God has given us His Spirit and the commands to preach biblical truth with humility and patience, in and out of season (2 Timothy 4:2), and to study to show ourselves approved workers who correctly handle the word of truth (2 Timothy 2:15). One day the Lord Jesus will return and put an end to all confusion.

Question: Why is the Bible called the "Holy Bible"?

Answer: The phrase *biblia sacra* ("holy books") first appeared sometime in the Middle Ages. In English, one of the earliest—if not *the* earliest—uses of "The Holy Bible" appeared in 1611 on the cover of the Authorized Version, known in the U.S. as the King James Version. The word *holy* has several meanings, and, as we will see, all of them describe the Word of God.

One meaning of *holy* is "sacred, sanctified, hallowed." When God spoke to Moses at the burning bush, He commanded him to remove his sandals because he was standing on "holy ground"— ground made holy by God's presence. Because God is sacred, the words He speaks are also sacred. In the same way, the words God gave Moses on Mount Sinai are sacred, as are all words God has given to mankind in the Bible. Since God is perfect, His words are perfect (Psalm 19:7). As God is righteous and pure, so is His Word (Psalm 19:8).

The Bible is holy because it was written by men under the direction and influence of the Holy Spirit. "All Scripture is God-breathed and is useful for teaching, rebuking, correcting and training in righteousness, so that the man of God may be thoroughly equipped for every good work" (2 Timothy 3:16–17). The Greek word translated "God-breathed" is *theopneustos*, from *theos*, meaning "God," and *pneo*, meaning "to breathe or breathe upon." So, our Holy God, in the person of the Holy Spirit, literally breathed the holy words of Scripture into the writers of each of the books of the Bible. The divine Writer is holy; therefore, what He writes is holy.

Another meaning of *holy* is "set apart." God set the nation of Israel apart from her contemporaries to be a "kingdom of priests and a holy nation" (Exodus 19:6). Similarly, Christians are set apart from unbelievers who walk in darkness, as described by Peter: "But you are a chosen people, a royal priesthood, a holy nation, a people belonging to God, that you may declare the praises of him who called you out of darkness into his wonderful light" (1 Peter 2:9). This "set apart" aspect of holiness is true of the Bible because it is a book set apart from all others. It is the only book written by God Himself, the only book that has the power to set men free (John 8:32), to change their lives and make them wise (Psalm 19:7), to sanctify them and make them holy (John 17:17). It is the only book that will endure forever (Matthew 5:18).

Question: What are the different names and titles of the Bible?

Answer: There are many names and titles of the Bible:

The Good Book—This name for the Bible is not found in the Bible itself; rather, it is an American colloquialism referring to the Bible. Since the Bible is "good" in every way, the name fits.

Holy Scriptures (Romans 1:2)—"The gospel he promised beforehand through his prophets in the Holy Scriptures." The Bible is a collection of sacred writings, which are holy and authoritative because God inspired them. Some translations of this verse have "Holy Writ" instead of "Holy Scriptures." A writ is simply "something written."

Law of the Lord (Psalm 19:7)—"The law of the LORD is perfect, reviving the soul. The statutes of the LORD are trustworthy, making wise the simple." The laws of the Bible are not to be confused with any other; they are the Lord's commands and the Lord's alone, not the ramblings of man.

Living Words (Acts 7:38)—"He was in the assembly in the desert, with the angel who spoke to him on Mount Sinai, and with our family; and he received living words to pass on to us." The Bible is a living book; each book, chapter, and verse is alive with the knowledge and wisdom of God Himself.

Scripture (2 Timothy 3:16)—"All Scripture is God-breathed and is useful for teaching, rebuking, correcting and training in righteousness." Inspired by God, the Bible is a collection of writings unlike any other. It is the only book written by men who were moved, or "carried along," by the Spirit of God (2 Peter 1:21).

The Scroll (Psalm 40:7)—"Here I am, I have come—it is written about me in the scroll." In this Messianic prophecy, the Bible is referred to as a scroll, a roll of parchment documenting priceless knowledge to be shared from generation to generation.

Sword of the Spirit (Ephesians 6:17)—"Take … the sword of the Spirit, which is the word of God." Like a sword, the Bible can parry any attack and pierce with the truth of God. It is the primary tool the Spirit uses to change a heart. The writer to the Hebrews says the Word of God is sharper than any "double-edged sword" because it is capable of "dividing soul and spirit, joints and marrow; it judges the thoughts and attitudes of the heart" (Hebrews 4:12).

Truth (John 17:17)—"Sanctify them by the truth; your word is truth." As the Bible is the Word of God, it is the truth. Every word is from the mind of God. Since He is truth, so must His Word be truth.

Word of God (Luke 11:28)—"Blessed rather are those who hear the word of God and obey it." The Bible is like the mouthpiece of God, as through each book He speaks directly to us. Often, this name is shortened to just "The Word."

Word of Life (Philippians 2:16)—"... hold out the word of life." The Bible reveals to us the difference between life and death—eternal life for those who accept Jesus Christ as their Savior and eternal death for those who do not.

Words of the Lord (Psalm 12:6)—"And the words of the LORD are flawless, like silver refined in a furnace of clay, purified seven times." The words of the Bible are perfect and without flaw because they are the words of the Lord, spoken through prophets and apostles to reveal God's love and glory.

Question: What is the sword of the Spirit?

Answer: The phrase "sword of the Spirit" is found only once in Scripture, in Ephesians 6:17, and refers to the Word of God. The sword is part of the spiritual armor Paul tells Christians to put on to enable us to fight effectively against evil (Ephesians 6:13).

The sword is both an offensive and defensive weapon used to protect oneself from harm or to attack the enemy and overcome him. When swords were used as the main weapons, it was necessary for a soldier to undergo rigid training on the proper use of a sword to get the maximum benefit from it. Since every Christian is in a spiritual battle against the satanic forces of this world, we need the same rigid training to know how to properly handle the sword of the Spirit, or God's Word. Only then will it be an effective defense against evil and a valuable offense to "demolish strongholds" of error and falsehood (2 Corinthians 10:4–5).

The Word is also called a sword in Hebrews 4:12. Here, the Word is described as living and active and sharper than a double-edged sword. A Roman sword was commonly double-edged, making it better for piercing and cutting both ways. The idea of Scripture "penetrating" means that the Word of God reaches the "heart," the very center of our nature, and lays open the motives and feelings of those it touches.

The purpose of the sword of the Spirit—the Bible—is to make us strong and enable us to withstand the onslaughts of Satan (Psalm 119:11, 33–40, 99–105). The Holy Spirit uses the power of the Word to save souls and give them spiritual strength to be mature soldiers for the Lord. The better we know the Word of God, the more useful we will be in accomplishing the will of God and the more effective in standing against the enemy of our souls.

Question: What are the most common things people think are in the Bible that are not actually in the Bible?

Answer: In Psalm 119:16, David promises God, "I delight in your decrees; I will not neglect your word." In Deuteronomy 11:18–19, God exhorts the Israelites, "Fix these words of mine in your hearts and minds; tie them as symbols on your hands and bind them on your foreheads. Teach them to your children, talking about them when you sit at home and when you walk along the road, when you lie down and when you get up." As believers, we know we are to study the Bible, memorize it, and obey it. But does the Bible say everything we *think* it says? The truth is, there are several phrases that sound like they come from the Bible, but do not.

"God helps those who
help themselves."

The earliest record of this saying is actually from Aesop's fable "Hercules and the Waggoner." A man's wagon gets stuck in a muddy road, and he prays for Hercules to help. Hercules appears and says, "Get up and put your shoulder to the wheel." The moral of the story is "The gods help them that help themselves." Aesop was a Greek writer who lived from 620 to 564 BC, but he obviously did not contribute to the Bible. Compared to biblical truth, the proverb is hit and miss. We can do nothing to help when it comes to salvation; salvation is through Christ alone. In the work of sanctification—becoming more spiritually mature—we are to join in the work. Faith is always accompanied by action (Hebrews 11), and the Bible condemns laziness (Proverbs 6:6).

"Cleanliness is next to godliness."

Despite the strict rules given to the Israelites about uncleanness and ceremonial washing (see the books of Exodus and Leviticus), this phrase is not in the Bible. It originated as an ancient Babylonian and Hebrew proverb, and it became very popular during the Victorian era after being revived by Sir Francis Bacon and John Wesley. Is it a true proverb? A new study shows that people are generally fairer and more generous when in a clean-smelling environment. And, of course, cleanliness has health benefits. But the Bible makes a careful distinction between external conditions and the condition of the heart. The rich man in Jesus' parable was undoubtedly clean, but he was far from godly (Luke 16:19–23).

"In the last days, you will not be able to know the seasons except by the changing of the leaves."

Evidently, this saying comes from "3 Days of Darkness," a prophecy of Padre Pio, a Roman Catholic priest. But it is not found in the Bible. Matthew 24:32–33 uses the budding of leaves heralding the coming of summer as a metaphor for the signs of Christ's return. But nowhere does the Bible mention that seasons will be so altered that only the changing leaves will identify them.

"It is better to cast your seed in the belly of a whore than to spill it out on the ground."

This saying is usually used to justify fornication or adultery over masturbation. It is one more misinterpretation of the story of Onan in Genesis 38:6–10. Onan's brother died, and Onan had the responsibility of marrying his brother's wife to provide an heir. Instead, Onan "spilled his semen on the ground to keep from producing offspring for his brother." This passage has nothing to do with masturbation or fornication; God struck Onan down because he selfishly refused to provide an heir for his deceased brother. In addition, the Bible would never encourage prostitution or any type of immorality. Instead, we are to control our physical appetites and remain faithful in marriage (1 Corinthians 6:12–20).

"Hate the sin, but love the sinner."

Although this is a biblical-sounding admonition, it is not from the Bible. It comes originally from Augustine, who said in one of his letters, "With love for mankind and hatred of sins" (*Letter 211*). The modern wording comes from a quote from Mahatma Gandhi. As a guideline, it's valid. God definitely loves sinners (Romans 5:8), and He has a holy hatred of sin (Isaiah 61:8). We are to hate sin—even our own. And we are to show love to all others. "Hating sin" is coming under fire today as more and more people define themselves by their sin and resent the guidelines God has given us in His Word.

"Money is the root of all evil."

This is a common misconception with an easy fix. First Timothy 6:10 actually says, "For *the love of* money is a root of all kinds of evil" (emphasis added). Money is not good or bad, and being wealthy is not a sin; Job was wealthy, yet was described as "blameless and upright; he feared God and shunned evil" (Job 1:1). *Loving* money, which in the Greek is "avarice" and implies an emotional affection, is the root of all sorts of evil, as the desire to accumulate wealth is placed above God and others.

"This too shall pass."

This is actually a paraphrase of a line from "The Lament of Deor," an Old English narrative poem. In the story, Deor has been replaced as his lord's minstrel, and he calls to mind several Germanic mythological figures who also went through troubled times. Each refrain ends with "that passed away, so may this." Several verses in the Bible remind us that our lives and, indeed, heaven and earth will pass away (e.g., Matthew 24:35). But, while we can find comfort in knowing that our earthly sorrows are temporary, we are still called to rejoice in our trials, knowing that they teach endurance and lead to sanctification (James 1:2–4).

"The lion shall lie down with the lamb."

This promise does not appear in the Bible, at least in these words. The animals are different. Isaiah 11:6 says, "The wolf will live with the lamb, the leopard will lie down with the goat, the calf and the lion and the yearling together; and a little child will lead them." Similarly, Isaiah 65:25 reads, "The wolf and the lamb will feed together, and the lion will eat straw like the ox." The sentiment reads true, however—predator and prey will be reconciled and live in peace in the future kingdom of God.

Some common sayings today are simple rewordings of biblical truth, but others are dangerous untruth. Despite how clever or even edifying a quote may be, if it isn't in the Bible, it is not the Word of God and therefore not a binding principle.

Question: What are the most famous/important questions in the Bible?

Answer: There are many, many questions in the Bible. It is difficult to give a precise number because ancient Hebrew and Koine Greek did not use punctuation—we can't just pull out the Dead Sea Scrolls and count the question marks! Often, it is difficult to know if a sentence is truly intended to be a question. But Bible scholars estimate that there are approximately 3,300 questions in the Bible.

This list of questions in the Bible is definitely not complete. It is simply a survey of some of the most famous and important questions in the Bible.

"Did God really say …?" (Genesis 3:1)

This is the first question in the Bible and also the first instance of someone questioning God's Word. Satan tempts Eve to doubt God's Word. Eve responds by adding to God's Word: "And you must not touch it" (Genesis 3:3). God said do not eat from the tree. He did not say, "Do not touch the tree or its fruit." Adam and Eve respond to Satan's question by disobeying God's Word. It went downhill from there—and it all started with a little question.

"Where are you?" (Genesis 3:9)

This is the first question asked by God in the Bible. Of course, God knew exactly where Adam and Eve were physically located. The question was for their benefit. God was essentially asking, "You disobeyed me; how is that working out for you? Did things turn out like you wanted or how I predicted?" The question also shows the heart of God, which is the heart of a shepherd seeking out the lost lambs in order to bring them into the fold. Jesus would later come "to seek and to save what was lost" (Luke 19:10).

"Am I my brother's keeper?" (Genesis 4:9)

This was Cain's question in response to God's question, "Where is your brother Abel?" Beyond the fact that Cain had just murdered his brother, Cain was expressing the feeling we all have when we do not want to care about or look after other people. Are we our brother's keeper? Yes, we are. Does this mean we have to know where they are and what they are doing 24/7? No. But, we should be invested enough in other people to notice when something seems to be out of place. We should care enough to intervene, if necessary.

"Will not the Judge of all the earth do right?" (Genesis 18:25)

Yes, the Judge of the earth always does right. Abraham asked this question in his appeal to God to spare the righteous and protect them from judgment. If something God does seems unjust, then we are misunderstanding it. When we question God's justice, it is because our sense of justice is warped. When we say, "I do not understand how a good and just God can allow such-and-such a thing," it is because we do not correctly understand what it means to be a good and just God. Many people think they have a better understanding of justice than God.

"Are you still holding on to your integrity? Curse God and die!" (Job 2:9)

The entire book of Job resounds with this question from Job's wife. Through it all, Job did maintain his integrity. Job's "friends" repeatedly say, "Job, you must have done something really bad for God to do this to you." God rebukes Job's friends for attacking Job and for presuming on God's sovereign will. Then God rebukes Job by reminding him that only God is perfect in all His ways. Included in God's presentation of His greatness are many questions: "Where were you when I laid the earth's foundation?" (Job 38:4).

"If a man dies, will he live again?" (Job 14:14)

Barring the return of Christ in our lifetimes, we will all die someday. Is there life after death? Everyone wonders about this question at some point. Yes, there is life after death, and everyone will experience it. It is simply a matter of *where* we will exist. Do all paths lead to God? In a way, yes. We will all stand before God after we die (Hebrews 9:27). No matter what path a man takes, he *will* meet God after death. "Multitudes who sleep in the dust of the earth will awake: some to everlasting life, others to shame and everlasting contempt" (Daniel 12:2).

"How can a young man keep his way pure?" (Psalm 119:9)

The answer: by living according to God's Word. When we "hide" God's Word in our hearts, the Word keeps us from sin (Psalm 119:11). The Bible does not tell us everything. It does not contain the answer to every question. But the Bible does tell us everything we need to know to live the Christian life (2 Peter 1:3). God's Word tells us our purpose and instructs us how to fulfill that purpose.

The Bible gives us the means and the end. God's Word is "useful for teaching, rebuking, correcting and training in righteousness, so that the man of God may be thoroughly equipped for every good work" (2 Timothy 3:16–17).

"Whom shall I send? And who will go for us?" (Isaiah 6:8)

Isaiah speaks the correct answer: "Here am I. Send me!" Far too often, our answer is, "Here am I—but send someone else." Isaiah 6:8 is a popular verse to use in connection with international missions. But, in context, God was not asking for someone to travel to the other side of the planet. God was asking for someone to deliver His message to the Israelites. God wanted Isaiah to declare the truth to the people he rubbed shoulders with every day—his own people, his family, his neighbors, his friends.

"Lord, how many times shall I forgive my brother when he sins against me? Up to seven times?" (Matthew 18:21)

Forgiveness is tough. Peter's suggestion of seven-fold forgiveness probably seemed, to him, to be superbly gracious. Jesus' answer showed how feeble our forgiveness usually is. We are to forgive because God has forgiven us of so much more (Colossians 3:13). We do not forgive because a person deserves it. "Deserve" has nothing to do with grace. We forgive because it is the right thing to do. That person might not deserve our forgiveness, but neither did we deserve God's, and He forgave us anyway.

"What shall I do, then, with Jesus?" (Matthew 27:22)

This was Pilate's question to the crowd gathered at Jesus' trial. Their answer: "Crucify Him!" Their shout a few days earlier had been different: "Hosanna to the Son of David! Blessed is he who comes in the name of the Lord!" (Matthew 21:9). It is amazing how unfulfilled expectations and a little peer pressure can change public opinion. In first-century Jerusalem, people who had an errant view of Jesus and His mission rejected Him; so, today, people who come to the Christian faith with an errant understanding of who Christ is will eventually turn away. We must be sure we accurately present who Jesus is and what Christianity is all about when we share our faith.

"Who do you say I am?"
(Matthew 16:15)

This question from Jesus is one of the most important a person will ever answer. For most people, Jesus is a good teacher. For some He is a prophet. For others He is a legend. Peter's answer, "You are the Christ, the Son of the living God" (Matthew 16:16), is the correct answer.

"What good is it for a man
to gain the whole world, yet
forfeit his soul?" (Mark 8:36)

If the cost is one's soul, then whatever is gained—even the whole world—is good for nothing. Sadly, "nothing" is what the vast majority of people strive after—the things of this world. To lose one's soul has two meanings. First, the more obvious meaning is that one loses his soul for eternity, experiencing eternal death in hell. However, seeking to gain the whole world will also cause you to lose your soul in a different way during this life. You will never experience the abundant life that is available through Jesus Christ (John 10:10). Solomon gave himself over to pleasure and denied himself nothing, yet he said, "Everything was meaningless, a chasing after the wind; nothing was gained" (Ecclesiastes 2:10–11).

"Good teacher, what must I do
to inherit eternal life?" (Luke

18:18) and "What must I do
to be saved?" (Acts 16:30)

It is interesting to see the very different responses of Jesus and Paul to what was essentially the same question. Jesus, knowing the self-righteous mindset of the rich young ruler, told him to obey the commandments. The man only *thought* he was righteous; Jesus knew that materialism and greed were preventing the man from truly seeking salvation. The man first needed to understand that he was a sinner in need of a Savior. Paul, recognizing that the Philippian jailer was ready to be saved, declared, "Believe in the Lord Jesus, and you will be saved." The jailer believed, and his family followed him in accepting Jesus as Savior. So, recognizing where a person is at in his or her spiritual journey can impact how we answer someone's questions and change the starting point in our presentation of the gospel.

"How can a man be born when he
is old? … Surely he cannot enter
a second time into his mother's
womb to be born!" (John 3:4)

Nicodemus asked this question when Jesus told him that he needed to be born again. People today still misunderstand what being born again means. Most everyone understands that being born again is not a reference to a second physical birth. However, most fail to understand the full implication of the term. Becoming a Christian—becoming born again—is beginning an entirely new life. It is moving from a state of spiritual death to a state of spiritual life (John 5:24). It is becoming a new creation (2 Corinthians 5:17). Being born again is not *adding* something to your existing life; it is radically *replacing* your existing life.

"Shall we go on sinning so that
grace may increase?" (Romans 6:1)

We are saved by grace (Ephesians 6:8). When we place our faith in Jesus Christ, all of our sins are forgiven and we are guaranteed eternal life in heaven. Salvation is God's gift of grace. Does this mean that a Christian can live however he or she wants and still be saved? Yes. *But* a true Christian will *not* live "however he or she wants." A Christian has a new Master and does not serve himself any more. A Christian will grow spiritually, progressively, in the new life God has given him. Grace is not a license to sin. Continuous willful, unrepentant sin in a person's life makes a mockery of grace and calls into question that person's salvation (1 John 3:6). Yes, there are times of failure and rebellion in a Christian's life. And, no, sinless perfection is not possible this side of glory. But the Christian is to live out of gratitude for God's grace, not take advantage of God's grace. The balance is found in Jesus' words to the woman caught in adultery. After refusing to condemn her, He said, "Go now and leave your life of sin" (John 8:11).

"If God is for us, who can be against us?" (Romans 8:31)

Children of God will face opposition in this world (John 15:18). The devil and his demons oppose us. Many people in the world oppose us. The philosophies, values, and priorities of the world stand against us. In terms of our earthly lives, we can be overcome, defeated, even killed. But in terms of eternity, God has promised that we will overcome (1 John 5:4). What is the worst thing that could possibly happen to us in this world? Death. For those who are born of God, what happens after death? Eternity in the most glorious place imaginable.

There are many other great questions in the Bible. Questions from seekers, questions from scoffers, questions from discouraged believers, and questions from God. Don't be afraid to ask questions, but be ready to accept God's answer when it comes.

Question: What is biblical numerology?

Answer: Biblical numerology is the study of numbers in the Bible. Two of the most commonly repeated numbers in the Bible are 7 and 40. The number 7 signifies completion or perfection (Genesis

7:2–4; Revelation 1:20). It is often called "God's number" since He is the only One who is perfect and complete (Revelation 4:5; 5:1, 5–6). The number 3 is also thought to be the number of divine perfection: the Trinity consists of Father, Son, and Holy Spirit.

The number *40* is often understood as the "number of probation or trial." For example, the Israelites wandered for 40 years (Deuteronomy 8:2–5); Moses was on the mount for 40 days (Exodus 24:18); Jonah warned Nineveh that judgment would fall after 40 days (Jonah 3:4); Jesus was tempted for 40 days (Matthew 4:2); there were 40 days between Jesus' resurrection and ascension (Acts 1:3). Another number repeated in the Bible is 4, which is the number of creation: north, south, east, west; four seasons. The number 6 is thought to be the number of man: man was created on the 6ᵗʰ day; man labors 6 days only. Another example of the Bible using a number to signify something is in Revelation 13:18, which says the number of the Antichrist is *666*.

Whether or not the numbers really have significance is still debated. The Bible definitely seems to use numbers in patterns or to teach spiritual truth. However, many people put too much significance on "biblical numerology," trying to find a special meaning behind every number in the Bible. Often, a number in the Bible is simply a number. God does not call us to search for secret meanings, hidden messages, or codes in the Bible. There is more than enough plain truth in Scripture to meet all our needs and make us "thoroughly equipped for every good work" (2 Timothy 3:17).

Question: What is the biblical significance of the number seven?

Answer: Throughout the Bible, God often gives symbolic significance to mundane items or concepts. For example, in Genesis 9:12–16, God makes the rainbow the sign of His promise to Noah (and, by extension, to all mankind) that He will not flood the whole earth again. God uses bread as a representation of His presence with His people (Numbers 4:7); of the gift of eternal life (John 6:35); and of the broken body of Christ, sacrificed for our sins (Matthew 26:26). The rainbow and the bread are obvious symbols in Scripture. Less obvious meanings seem to be attached to some numbers in the Bible, especially the number 7, which at times provides a special emphasis in the text.

The first use of the number 7 in the Bible relates to the creation week in Genesis 1—2. God spends six days creating the heavens and the earth, and then rests on the seventh day. This is our template for the seven-day week, observed around the world to this day. The seventh day was to be "set apart" for Israel; the Sabbath was a holy day of rest (Deuteronomy 5:12).

Thus, right at the start of the Bible, the number 7 is identified with something being "finished" or "complete." From then on, that association continues, as 7 is often found in contexts involving completeness or divine perfection. So we see the command for animals to be at least seven days old before being used for sacrifice (Exodus 22:30), the command for leprous Naaman to bathe in the Jordan River seven times to effect complete cleansing (2 Kings 5:14), and the command for Joshua to march around Jericho for seven days (and on the seventh day to make seven circuits) and for seven priests to blow seven trumpets outside the city walls (Joshua 6:3–4). In these instances, 7 signifies a completion of some kind: a divine mandate is fulfilled.

Interestingly, man was created on the sixth day of creation. In some passages of the Bible, the number 6 is associated with mankind. In Revelation "the number of the beast" is called "the number of a man. That number is 666" (Revelation 13:18). If God's number is 7, then man's is 6. Six always falls short of seven, just like "all have sinned and fall short of the glory of God" (Romans 3:23). Man is not God, just as 6 is not 7.

Series of seven things crop up often in the Bible. For example, we find seven pairs of each clean animal on the ark (Genesis 7:2); seven stems on the tabernacle's lampstand (Exodus 25:37); seven qualities of the Messiah in Isaiah 11:2; seven signs in John's gospel; seven things the Lord hates in Proverbs 6:16; seven parables in Matthew 13; and seven woes in Matthew 23.

Multiples of 7 also figure into the biblical narrative: the "seventy sevens" prophecy in Daniel 9:24 concerns 490 years (7 times 7 times 10). Jeremiah 29:10 predicted the Israelite captivity in Babylon would last for seventy years (7 times 10). According to Leviticus 25:8, the Year of Jubilee was to begin after the passing of every forty-ninth year (7 times 7).

Sometimes, the symbolism of 7 is a great comfort to us: Jesus is the seven-fold "I AM" in the gospel of John. Other times, it challenges us: Jesus told Peter to forgive a wrongdoer "seventy times seven" times (Matthew 18:22 NKJV). And then there are passages in which the number 7 is associated with God's judgment: the seven bowls of the great tribulation, for example (Revelation 16:1) or God's warning to Israel in Leviticus 26:18.

Speaking of the book of Revelation, the number 7 is used there more than fifty times in a variety of contexts: there are seven letters to seven churches in Asia and seven spirits before God's throne (Revelation 1:4), seven golden lampstands (1:12), seven stars in Christ's right hand (1:16), seven seals of God's judgment (5:1), seven angels with seven trumpets (8:2), etc. In all likelihood, the number 7 again represents completeness or totality: the seven churches represent the completeness of the body of Christ, the seven seals on the scroll represent the fullness of God's punishment of a sinful earth, and so on. And, of course, the book of Revelation itself, with all its 7s, is the capstone of God's Word to man. With the book of Revelation, the Word was complete.

In all, the number 7 is used in the Bible more than 700 times. If we include the words related to *seven* (terms like *sevenfold* or *seventy* or *seven hundred*), the count is still higher. Of course, not every instance of the number 7 in the Bible carries a deeper significance. Sometimes, a 7 is just a 7, and we must be cautious about attaching symbolic meanings to any text, especially when Scripture is not explicit about such meanings. However, there are times when it *seems* that God is communicating the idea of divine completeness, perfection, and wholeness by means of the number 7.

Question: Does the warning in Revelation 22:18–19 apply to the entire Bible or just to the book of Revelation?

Answer: Revelation 22:18–19 contains a warning to anyone who tampers with the biblical text: "I warn everyone who hears the words of the prophecy of this book: If anyone adds anything to them, God will add to him the plagues described in this book. And if anyone takes words away from this book of prophecy, God will take away from him his share in the tree of life and in the holy city, which are described in this book." Do these verses refer to the whole Bible or just to the book of Revelation?

This warning is given specifically to those who distort the message of the book of Revelation. Jesus Himself is the author of Revelation and the giver of the vision to the apostle John (Revelation 1:1). As such, He concludes the book by confirming the finality of the prophecies. These are His words, and He warns against distorting them in any way, whether through additions, subtractions, falsifications, alterations, or intentional misinterpretations. The warning is explicit and dire. The plagues of Revelation will be visited upon anyone guilty of tampering with the revelations in the book, and those who do so will have no part of eternal life in heaven.

Although the warning in Revelation 22:18–19 is specific to the book of Revelation, the principle behind it applies to anyone who intentionally distorts God's Word. Moses gave a similar warning in Deuteronomy 4:1–2, where he cautioned the Israelites to listen to and obey the commandments of the Lord, neither adding to nor taking away from His Word. Proverbs 30:5–6 contains a similar admonition to anyone who would add to God's words: he will be rebuked and proven to be a liar. We must be careful to handle the Bible with care and reverence so as to not distort its message.

Question: What are the modern equivalents of biblical weights and measures?

Answer: The use of weights and measurements was common in ancient times, just like it is today. The problem is that the words used for various measurements were usually specific to that culture.

Today, most people don't know what a "shekel" is or the difference between a "furlong" and a "fathom." Some Bible translations have replaced the archaic words with modern equivalents or approximations. Other translations simply transliterate the Greek and Hebrew words for the measurements.

Below are several terms and their approximated equivalents in both metric and imperial measurements. Since some ancient terms varied by area, we have differentiated Greek and Hebrew measurements.

Weights

- Hebrew
  - Talent (3,000 shekels or 60 minas, sometimes translated "100 pounds")
    - 34.272 kg/75.6 lbs
  - Mina (50 shekels, sometimes translated "pound")
    - 571.2 g/1.26 lbs
  - Shekel
    - 11.424 g/0.403 oz
  - Pim (⅔ shekel)
    - 7.616 g/0.258 oz
  - Beca (½ shekel)
    - 5.712 g/.201 oz
  - Gerah (.02 shekel)
    - 0.571 g/0.02 oz
- Greek
  - Litra (30 shekels, sometimes translated "pound")
    - 0.4 kg/12 oz
  - Talent
    - 40 kg/88 lbs
  - Mina
    - 571.2 g/1.26 lbs

Linear Measurements

- Hebrew
  - Reed (6 cubits)
    - 2.7 m/8¾ ft or 3 yds

- ○ Cubit (2 spans, sometimes translated "yard," "half a yard," or "foot")
  - ▪ 0.5 m/18 in
- ○ Span (½ cubit or 3 handbreadths)
  - ▪ 23 cm/9 in
- ○ Handbreadth (⅙ cubit, span, or 4 fingers, sometimes translated "3 or 4 inches")
  - ▪ 8 cm/3 in
- ○ Finger
  - ▪ 1.8 cm/0.73 in
- Ezekiel's Cubit (found in Ezekiel 40:5)
  - ○ Reed (6 of Ezekiel's cubits)
    - ▪ 3.1 m/10 ft, 2.4 in
  - ○ Cubit (7 handbreadths)
    - ▪ 0.5 m/20.4 in
- Greek
  - ○ Milion (8 stadia, sometimes translated "mile")
    - ▪ 1.5 km/1,620 yds or 0.9 mi
  - ○ Stadion (⅛ milion or 400 cubits, sometimes translated "mile," "furlong," or "race")
    - ▪ 185 m/⅛ mi
  - ○ Kalamos (6 cubits, sometimes translated "rod," "reed," or "measuring rod")
    - ▪ 3 m/3⅓ yds
  - ○ Fathom (4 cubits, sometimes translated "6 feet")
    - ▪ 2 m/2 yds
  - ○ Cubit (sometimes translated "yard," "half a yard," or "foot")
    - ▪ 0.5 m/18 in

Dry Measures

- Hebrew
  - ○ Kor (10 ephahs, sometimes translated "cor," "homer," "sack," "measures," "bushels")
    - ▪ 220 L/5.16 bsh or 200 qts

- Letek (5 ephahs, sometimes translated "half homer" or "half sack")
  - 110 L/2.68 bsh
- Ephah/Bath (10 omers, sometimes translated "bushel," "peck," "deal," "part," "measure," or "6 or 7 pints")
  - 22 L/³⁄₅ bsh
- Seah (⅓ ephah, sometimes translated "measure," "peck," or "large amount")
  - 7.3 L/7 qts
- Omer/Issaron (.1 ephah, sometimes translated "tenth of a deal" or "six pints")
  - 2 L/2.09 qts
- Cab (.056 ephah, sometimes translated "cab")
  - 1 L/1 qt

Greek

- Koros (10 ephahs, sometimes translated "sack," "measure," "bushel," or "500 quartsbus")
  - 525 L/14.9 bsh
- Modios (4 omers, sometimes translated "bushel," "bowl," "peck," "corn-measure," or "meal-tub")
  - 9 L/1 pk or ¼ bsh
- Saton (⅓ ephah, sometimes translated "measure," "peck," or "large amount")
  - 7.3 L/7 qts
- Choinix (.056 ephah, sometimes translated "measure" or "quart")
  - 1 L/1 qt
- Xestes (½ cab, sometimes translated "pot," "pitcher," "kettle," "copper bowl," or "vessels of bronze")
  - 0.5 L/1⅙ pts

Liquid Measures

- Hebrew
  - Cor / Homer

- 208 L/55 gal
  - Bath (1 ephah, sometimes translated "gallon," "barrel," or "liquid measure")
    - 22 L/5.5 gal
  - Hin (⅙ bath, sometimes translated "pints")
    - 4 L/1 gal (4 qts)
  - Log (.72 bath, sometimes translated "pint" or "cotulus")
    - 0.3 L/0.67 pt
- Greek
  - Metretes (10 hins, sometimes translated "firkins" or "gallons")
    - 39 L/10 gal
  - Batos (1 ephah, sometimes translated "gallon," "barrel," or "measure")
    - 22 L/6 gal
  - Xestes (⅛ hin, sometimes translated "pot," "pitcher," "kettle," "copper bowl," or "vessel of bronze")
    - 0.5 L/1⅙ pts

Coins and Monies

- Denarius/Denarion: a day's wage ("penny" in the KJV)
- Daric/Drachma/Dram: a coin weighing ¼ oz or 8.5 g
- Lepta: the smallest Greek copper coin; of unknown weight (translated "mite" in the KJV)
- Kodrantess: the smallest Roman copper coin; of unknown weight (translated "mite" in the KJV)

Question: What is bibliolatry?

Answer: The term *bibliolatry* comes from combining the Greek words for *book* and *worship*. In a Christian context, bibliolatry is, simply stated, the worship of the Bible. Typically, the accusation of bibliolatry is used as an attack on those who believe in the inerrancy, infallibility, and supremacy of Scripture as well as those who hold to a literal interpretation of the Bible.

It is important to note that the charge of bibliolatry does not claim some Christians literally bow down before a Bible and worship it as if it were an idol. While there may be some strange cult out there that literally worships the Bible that way, that is not what *bibliolatry* is referring to. The accusation of bibliolatry is that some Christians elevate the Bible to the point that it is equal with God, or to the point that studying the Bible is more important than developing a personal and intimate relationship with Jesus Christ.

First, it is important to understand what the Bible says about itself. Second Timothy 3:16–17 declares, "All Scripture is God-breathed and is useful for teaching, rebuking, correcting and training in righteousness, so that the man of God may be thoroughly equipped for every good work." So, if the Bible is "God-breathed," and God does not lie (Titus 1:2), then every word in the Bible must be true. Believing in an inerrant, infallible, and authoritative Bible is not bibliolatry. Rather, it is simply believing what the Bible says about itself. Further, believing what the Bible says about itself is in fact worshipping the God who breathed out His Word. A perfect, infallible, omnipotent, omnipresent, and omniscient God would create written revelation that is itself perfect and infallible.

Do some believers emphasize the Bible to the point that other things of importance—such as tradition, nature, reason, and experience—are neglected? Yes. However, the Bible, if it is the Word of God, must be a higher authority than any of these and must, in fact, be the authority by which they are judged. The Bible is not to be worshipped, but the God of the Bible is. To ignore what God has revealed about Himself in His Word and instead elevate the subjective "revelations" of nature, reason, and experience is idolatry (Romans 1:18–25).

The Bible is not God. But it is His Word and is therefore "perfect … trustworthy … right … radiant … sure … righteous … precious" (Psalm 19:7–10). The Bible is "holy" because God is (2 Timothy 3:15). The Bible is not "more important" than a personal relationship with Christ, but it is necessary to understand the Bible in order to know who Christ is. The Bible is about the Lord Jesus (Luke 24:27). It is through the Bible that the Lord is revealed: "You diligently study the Scriptures because you think that by them you possess eternal life. These are the Scriptures that testify about me" (John 5:39). Without the Word of God, we cannot have faith in Christ: "Faith comes from hearing the message, and the message is heard through the word of Christ" (Romans 10:17).

The accusation of "Bible-worship" comes from those with a low view of Scripture who want to either add to or subtract from what God has said. We do not worship a leather-bound book, but the Bible must be our authority, and we must use it to test the conclusions we reach with our God-given reason and God-directed experience (1 Peter 3:15). Believing what the Bible says about itself is not bibliolatry. Rather, accepting God's Word for what it claims to be is in fact worshipping the God who breathed it.

Appendix—
Statement of Faith

Section 1: The Bible

We believe the Bible, comprised of the Old and New Testaments, to be the inspired, infallible, and authoritative Word of God (Matthew 5:18; 2 Timothy 3:16–17). In faith we hold the Bible to be inerrant in the original writings, God-breathed, and the complete and final authority for faith and practice (2 Timothy 3:16–17). While still using the individual writing styles of the human authors, the Holy Spirit perfectly guided them to ensure they wrote precisely what He wanted written, without error or omission (2 Peter 1:21).

Section 2: God

We believe in one God, who is Creator of all (Deuteronomy 6:4; Colossians 1:16), who has revealed Himself in three distinct Persons—Father, Son, and Holy Spirit (2 Corinthians 13:14), yet who is one in being, essence, and glory (John 10:30). God is eternal (Psalm 90:2), infinite (1 Timothy 1:17), and sovereign (Psalm 93:1).

God is omniscient (Psalm 139:1–6), omnipresent (Psalm 139:7–13), omnipotent (Revelation 19:6), and unchanging (Malachi 3:6). God is holy (Isaiah 6:3), just (Deuteronomy 32:4), and righteous (Exodus 9:27). God is love (1 John 4:8), gracious (Ephesians 2:8), merciful (1 Peter 1:3), and good (Romans 8:28).

Section 3: Jesus Christ

We believe in the deity of the Lord Jesus Christ. He is God incarnate, God in human form—the expressed image of the Father, who, without ceasing to be God, became man in order that He might demonstrate who God is and provide the means of salvation for humanity (Matthew 1:21; John 1:18; Colossians 1:15).

We believe that Jesus Christ was conceived of the Holy Spirit and was born of the virgin Mary (Matthew 1:23); that He is truly fully God and truly fully man (John 1:1, 14); that He lived a perfect, sinless life (Hebrews 4:15); and that all His teachings are true. We believe that the Lord Jesus Christ died on the cross for all humanity (1 John 2:2) as a substitutionary sacrifice (Isaiah 53:5–6). We hold that His death is sufficient to provide salvation for all who receive Him as Savior (John 1:12; Acts 16:31); that our justification is grounded in the shedding of His blood (Romans 5:9); and that it is attested by His literal, physical resurrection from the dead (Matthew 28:6; 1 Peter 1:3).

We believe that the Lord Jesus Christ ascended to heaven in His glorified body (Acts 1:9–11) and is now seated at the right hand of God as our High Priest and Advocate (Romans 8:34; Hebrews 4:14).

Section 4: The Holy Spirit

We believe in the deity and personality of the Holy Spirit (Acts 5:3–4). He regenerates sinners (Titus 3:5) and indwells believers (Romans 8:9). He is the agent by whom Christ baptizes all believers into His body (1 Corinthians 12:12–14). He is the seal by whom the Father guarantees the salvation of believers unto the day of redemption (Ephesians 1:13–14). He is the Divine Teacher who

212

illumines believers' hearts and minds as they study the Word of God (1 Corinthians 2:9–12).

We believe that the Holy Spirit is ultimately sovereign in the distribution of spiritual gifts (1 Corinthians 12:8–11). We believe that the miraculous gifts of the Spirit, while by no means outside of the Spirit's ability to empower, no longer function to the same degree they did in the early development of the church (1 Corinthians 12:4–11; 2 Corinthians 12:12; Ephesians 2:20; 4:7–12).

Section 5: Angels and Demons

We believe in the reality and personality of angels. We believe that God created the angels to be His servants and messengers (Nehemiah 9:6; Psalm 148:2; Hebrews 1:14).

We believe in the existence and personality of Satan and demons. Satan is a fallen angel who led a group of angels in rebellion against God (Isaiah 14:12–17; Ezekiel 28:12–15). He is the great enemy of God and man, and the demons are his servants in evil. He and his demons will be eternally punished in the lake of fire (Matthew 25:41; Revelation 20:10).

Section 6: Humanity

We believe that humanity came into existence by direct creation of God and that humanity is uniquely made in the image and likeness of God (Genesis 1:26–27). We believe that all humanity, because of Adam's fall, has inherited a sinful nature; that all human beings choose to sin (Romans 3:23); and that all sin is exceedingly offensive to God (Romans 6:23). Humanity is utterly unable to remedy this fallen state (Ephesians 2:1–5, 12).

Section 7: Salvation

We believe that salvation is a gift of God's grace through faith in the finished work of Jesus Christ on the cross (Ephesians 2:8–9). Christ's death fully accomplished justification through faith and redemption from sin. Christ died in our place (Romans 5:8–9) and bore our sins in His own body (1 Peter 2:24).

We believe salvation is received by grace alone, through faith alone, in Christ alone. Good works and obedience are results of salvation, not requirements for salvation. Due to the greatness, sufficiency, and perfection of Christ's sacrifice, all those who have truly received Christ as Savior are eternally secure in salvation, kept by God's power, and secured and sealed in Christ forever (John 6:37–40; 10:27–30; Romans 8:1, 38–39; Ephesians 1:13–14; 1 Peter 1:5; Jude 24). Just as salvation cannot be earned by good works, neither does it need good works to be maintained or sustained. Good works and changed lives are the inevitable results of salvation (James 2:14–26).

Section 8: The Church

We believe that the church, the body of Christ, is a spiritual organism made up of all believers of this present age (1 Corinthians 12:12–14; Ephesians 1:22–23; 5:25–27). We believe in the ordinances of believers' water baptism by immersion as a testimony to Christ and identification with Him, and the Lord's Supper as a remembrance of Christ's death and shed blood (Matthew 28:19–20; Acts 2:41–42; 18:8; 1 Corinthians 11:23–26). Through the church, believers are to be taught to obey the Lord and to testify concerning their faith in Christ as Savior and to honor Him by holy living. We believe in the Great Commission as the primary mission of the Church. It is the obligation of all believers to witness, by word and life, to the truths of God's Word. The gospel of the grace of God is to be preached to all the world (Matthew 28:19–20; Acts 1:8; 2 Corinthians 5:19–20).

Section 9: Things to Come

We believe in the blessed hope (Titus 2:13), the personal and imminent coming of the Lord Jesus Christ to rapture His saints (1 Thessalonians 4:13–17). We believe in the visible and bodily return of Christ to the earth with His saints to establish His promised millennial kingdom (Zechariah 14:4–11; 1 Thessalonians 1:10; Revelation 20:1–6). We believe in the physical resurrection of all men—the saints to everlasting joy and bliss on the New Earth, and the wicked to eternal punishment in the lake of fire (Matthew 25:46; John 5:28–29; Revelation 20:5–6, 12–13).

We believe that the souls of believers are, at death, absent from the body and present with the Lord, where they await their resurrection when spirit, soul, and body are reunited to be glorified forever with the Lord (Luke 23:43; 2 Corinthians 5:8; Philippians 1:23; 3:21). We believe that the souls of unbelievers remain, after death, in conscious misery until their resurrection when, with soul and body reunited, they shall appear at the Great White Throne judgment and shall be cast into the lake of fire to suffer everlasting punishment (Matthew 25:41–46; Mark 9:43–48; Luke 16:19–26; 2 Thessalonians 1:7–9; Revelation 20:11–15).

ENDNOTES

1   Dan Brown, *The Da Vinci Code* (New York: Anchor, 2003).

2   Dan Burstein, *Secrets of the Code: The Unauthorized Guide to the Mysteries Behind The Da Vinci Code* (New York: Vanguard Press, 2004).

3   Frederic G. Kenyon, *The Bible and Archaeology* (New York: Harper & Brothers, 1940).

4   Frederic G. Kenyon, Ed. by A.W. Adams, *Our Bible And The Ancient Manuscripts: Being A History Of The Text And Its Translations* (New York: Harper & Row, 1958).

5   Donald S. Whitney, *Spiritual Disciplines for the Christian Life* (Carol Stream, Illinois: Tyndale House Publishers, Inc., 1997).

6   John Adams, L. H. Butterfield, Leonard C. Faber and Wendell D. Garrett, *Diary and Autobiography of John Adams, Volumes 1–4* (Cambridge, Massachusetts: Belknap Press, 1961).

SCRIPTURE INDEX

Romans

1 Corinthians

Made in the USA
Middletown, DE
11 May 2016